Harvey Cushing 1869–1939

TRADITION, INDEED, IS THE MOST powerful binding influence the world knows. It lies deep in most of us, and pride in tradition supplies the glue which holds people and groups of people in cohesion. Pride in family and friends, in Alma Mater and profession, in race and birthplace, in state and nation. The controlling subconsciousness of one's stock and upbringing is something from which time and distance can never wholly wean us.

Harvey Cushing

HISTORY OF
the AMERICAN ASSO
of NEUR

American
Association of
Neurological
Surgeons

ATION

OLOGICAL

SURGEONS

SEVENTY–FIFTH ANNIVERSARY

FOUNDED IN 1931 AS
THE HARVEY CUSHING SOCIETY

THE
DONNING COMPANY
PUBLISHERS

For information, write:
The American Association of Neurological Surgeons
5550 Meadowbrook Drive
Rolling Meadows, Illinois 60008-3852

Library of Congress Cataloging-in-Publication Data

American Association of Neurological Surgeons.
   History of the American Association of Neurological Surgeons, seventy–fifth anniversary : founded in 1931 as the Harvey Cushing Society / by the American Association of Neurological Surgeons.
      p. ; cm.
   Includes bibliographical references.
   ISBN–13: 978–1–57864–403–2
   ISBN–10: 1–57864–403–8
   1. Neurosurgeons—Biography. 2. Nervous system—Surgery—History. I. Title.
   [DNLM: 1. Harvey Cushing Society. 2. American Association of Neurological Surgeons. 3. Neurosurgery—history. 4. Societies, Medical—history. 5. History, 20th Century. 6. History, 21st Century. WL 1 A5115h 2007]
   RD592.8.A45 2007
   617.4'8009—dc22

                                                                                    2006035888

Produced by:
The Donning Company Publishers
184 Business Park Drive, Suite 206
Virginia Beach, VA 23462–6533

Printed in the United States of America by Walsworth Publishing Company

TABLE OF CONTENTS

‖ Preface ‖

Eugene S. Flamm, MD
AANS Historian

IN THE PAST 25 YEARS SINCE THE LAST major anniversary of the AANS, the Association has undergone many changes. This recent period has seen far greater development than in the first 50 years, except for the founding of the Harvey Cushing Society and the change of name to AANS. The essays that described the early developments have been reprinted in this, the 75th Anniversary Volume.

The transformation of a small, perhaps elitist club—the Harvey Cushing Society—into a national and international organization that is the voice of neurosurgery throughout the world is the major development of the past 25 years. This is reflected in the scope of activities which are summarized in this volume. Major developments have been the expansion of the *Journal of Neurosurgery (JNS)* and the extraordinary growth of the Neurosurgery Research and Education Foundation (NREF), which are addressed by Drs. Jane and Weiss. The listings of the special awards and special lecturers are indicative of the growth of the organization over this period. This is also reflected in the increase in membership in this organization, which began with 23 individuals with direct connections to Harvey Cushing in 1932 and has increased to more than 7,000 members today around the world, for whom Harvey Cushing may be no more than a mythical name.

In addition to its mission to represent neurosurgery throughout the world, the educational mission of the Association has continued to widen. The annual meetings, the postgraduate courses, the publications and the political representation of the interests of neurosurgery have characterized the past 25 years. The responsibility of the AANS for the future of neurosurgery is perhaps no better demonstrated than in the prominence that has been achieved by the NREF, funded by the shared belief of our members in the importance of research for the future of neurosurgery as an intellectual discipline.

How these activities will change over the next 25 years is difficult to predict. What is certain is that in 2032, when we celebrate the 100th anniversary of our founding, many activities that now capture the attention of neurosurgeons will have disappeared, only to be replaced by some which we can only begin to imagine today. The growth in size and scope of the AANS in its first 75 years should give us assurance that we will meet the challenges of the next 25 years.

THE HARVEY CUSHING SOCIETY

THIRTY-SECOND ANNUAL MEETING
HOTEL AMBASSADOR
ANGELES, CALIFORNIA
21, 22, 1964

THE AMERICAN ASSOCIATION
OF NEUROLOGICAL SURGEONS

founded in 1931 as
The Harvey Cushing Society

THIRTY-NINTH ANNUAL MEETING
SHAMROCK-HILTON HOTEL
HOUSTON, TEXAS
APRIL 18–21, 1971

The Astrodome

AANS

Scientific Program

The 59th Annual Meeting
of the
American Association of Neurological Surgeons
April 20-25, 1991

NORTH OF BOSTON

SCIENTIFIC PROGRAM

The 61st Annual Meeting
American Association of Neurological Surgeons
April 24-29, 1993

‖ Acknowledgments ‖

THE AANS WOULD LIKE TO ACKNOWLEDGE the work of Francine T. Byrnes, Betsy van Die, and Kathleen Craig in the development of this book. Special thanks to Chris Ann Philips, who has served as the AANS Archivist since 1989.

HARVEY CUSHING
and the
FOUNDING
of the
HARVEY CUSHING
SOCIETY

PAUL C. BUCY, MD

Reprinted from *History of the American Association of Neurological Surgeons Founded in 1931 as The Harvey Cushing Society, 1931–1981*

THE PARTICIPATION OF HARVEY CUSHING IN the formation and organization of the Harvey Cushing Society was a varied one. It was not his idea, and he did not arrange for the early meetings of the organization as he did for the Society of Neurological Surgeons. On the other hand, he encouraged R. Glen Spurling and William P. Van Wagenen, who were the prime movers in creating this new society. He recognized that the Society of Neurological Surgeons was closed to many of the younger men and that they needed a society where they could meet and exchange ideas. Once Drs. Spurling and Van Wagenen had met and recruited Temple Fay and Eustace Semmes to join with them in this new venture, Dr. Cushing invited them to hold the first

meeting of the Harvey Cushing Society with him in Boston. He also gave his approval of their naming the new society after him.

Twenty-three people attended that first meeting on May 6, 1932. However, there are only 21 people in the photograph of the group. One of the other two was Richard Upjohn Light, who took the picture, but I have been unable to learn who the other person was. Of these 22, only six had been neurosurgical residents under Dr. Cushing: Tracy J. Putnam, Franc D. Ingraham, Leo M. Davidoff, William P. Van Wagenen, William J. German, and Eric Oldberg. Glen Spurling had been a house officer at the Peter Bent Brigham Hospital but not on Dr. Cushing's service. Louise Eisenhardt had been Dr. Cushing's secretary and later his neuropathologist. Merrill C. Sosman had been Dr. Cushing's radiologist. The others had had their training elsewhere. Accordingly, the Harvey Cushing Society was never just an association of Cushing people. As time passed, the proportion of non-Cushing neurosurgeons steadily rose. Nevertheless, the opinion that the Harvey Cushing Society was merely a private club of Cushing people persisted even in some important quarters such as the National

> *At the first meeting of the Harvey Cushing Society in Boston on May 6, 1932, Harvey Cushing was a most gracious and affable host.*

Opposite page: Attendees at the first annual meeting of the Harvey Cushing Society held at the Peter Bent Brigham Hospital, May 6, 1932.

Back Row *(left to right)*: R. Glen Spurling, R. Eustace Semmes, Temple Fay, Eric Oldberg, Stafford Warren, William J. German, W. Edward Chamberlain, James G. Lyerly, Merrill C. Sosman, William P. Van Wagenen, Frank Fremont-Smith, Leo M. Davidoff, Roland M. Klemme, Frank R. Teachenor.

Front Row: Edgar A. Kahn, Paul C. Bucy, Franc D. Ingraham, Louise Eisenhardt, John F. Fulton, Tracy J. Putnam, Franklin Jelsma.

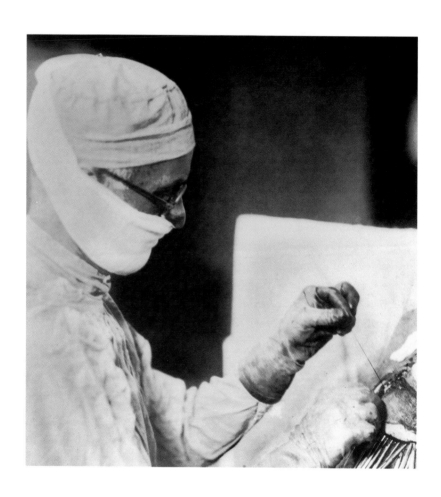

Institutes of Health. It thus became necessary to change the name of the organization to remove this misunderstanding.

At the first meeting of the Harvey Cushing Society in Boston on May 6, 1932, Harvey Cushing was a most gracious and affable host. He performed a memorable operation which was both difficult and amazingly successful. He resected a glioma from the wall of the third ventricle. The evening of the day of the operation, Dr. Cushing showed this patient to the group. John Fulton records in his biography of Harvey Cushing, "She was married a short time later and is still living and well, with a family of two children (November 1945)." What a stimulating demonstration of the superb surgical ability of the man whom the new society honored. As Dr. Cushing himself wrote shortly after this meeting, "I am very proud of you all and that I should have been immortalized by having you use my name is a source of pride and gratification."

The Harvey Cushing Society may not have been Dr. Cushing's idea, but he certainly got it off to an impressive start and provided it every support that he could.

For a list of charter members, see Page 80.

The Harvey Cushing Society, April 1942, New York City, New York

HISTORY *of the* HARVEY CUSHING SOCIETY

1931–1965

EBEN ALEXANDER JR., MD

Reprinted from *History of the American Association of Neurological Surgeons Founded in 1931 as the Harvey Cushing Society, 1931–1981*

THE FIRST OFFICIAL MEETING OF THE Harvey Cushing Society was held in Boston, Massachusetts, May 6, 1932. The formation of this society was stimulated by the need, keenly felt by the younger neurosurgeons of that day, for contact with their colleagues in order to effect an exchange of ideas that would advance their knowledge and improve their skills in their chosen field.

It was Dr. Temple Fay who first suggested that the Society be named in honor of Dr. Harvey Cushing, and all of those who first initiated the formation of the organization agreed that this would be most suitable.

Much of the actual initiation of this movement was the work of Dr. R. Glen Spurling, who wrote Dr. William P. Van Wagenen, arranging a preliminary meeting which was held in Washington, D.C., at the Hotel Raleigh, October 10, 1931; Dr. Spurling, Dr. Van Wagenen, Dr. Fay, and Dr. Eustace Semmes were in attendance.

Record of the Meeting Held in Washington on October 10, 1931, at the Hotel Raleigh

> *"Drs. Spurling, Semmes, Fay and Van Wagenen met for the purpose of considering the advisability of forming a new society for the purpose of study and advancement and correlation of subjects relating to organic neurology, such subjects being, neurosurgery, medical neurology as practiced today, neurophysiology, neuropathology and roentgenology."*

> *"In general, it was thought worthwhile and advisable to form such a society. A list of names was suggested and temporarily acted upon as men to whom invitations would be sent."*

"It was also thought advisable to consider the forming of a central library for filing and interpretation of sections of brain tumors of unusual interest."

"In order that there could not be any confusion of the aims of this society with those of the existing neurosurgical society, it was thought advisable to consult with Dr. Cushing who is the founder of the present neurosurgical society and with Dr. Coleman who is the president of that society this year. Dr. Spurling was to see Dr. Coleman and Dr. Van Wagenen was to see Dr. Cushing."

"Various names were suggested for the society which were: 1. Cushing Society; 2. Cushing Research Society; 3. Cushing Neurosurgical Society; 4. Cushing Society for Study and Advancement of Organic Neurology; 6. Cushing Round Table of Organic Neurology."

"It was also decided that the society might have one meeting a year to be limited to three days; that the first day should be in the hands of the man in whose clinic the meeting was held and that the next two days should be given over to the discussion of work of the individual members and that the policy of inviting guests outside of the society for the presentation of papers might well be adhered to."

"It was also thought that an advisable policy might be to apportion research problems among various clinics with a time limit of two years or so to report on them."

"It was also decided that membership in general should be a fairly wide one and that as time goes on younger men might gain admission to the society either by invitation of the society or through the filing of application which of course would be acted upon by an executive committee."

W. P. Van Wagenen, MD

The Harvey Cushing Society Annual Dinner, May 1937, Philadelphia, Pennsylvania

The Harvey Cushing Society, April 1938, Memphis, Tennessee

Charter Members (see Page 80) were selected, and Dr. Cushing was advised of the proposed formation of the new group. He, in turn, issued an invitation to the organization to hold its first meeting at his clinic in Boston.

Initially, the purpose of the society was the promotion and advancement of various fields of organic neurology, and the membership included not only neurosurgeons but those in the fields of neurology, neuroanatomy, neuro-ophthalmology, neuropathology, psychiatry, psychology, roentgenology, and other scientific disciplines bearing on neurosurgery. Subsequently, as the organization has grown, the Active Membership has been made up of neurosurgeons, and members of allied fields have constituted the Associate Membership.

In order that a close contact might be maintained between members and a free exchange of ideas encouraged, the membership originally was limited to 35.

Dr. Cushing conducted an operative clinic at the first meeting and demonstrated a number of patients to the assembled group during the meeting. Dr. Fay suggested that the new society be named for Dr. Cushing, and his suggestion was accepted. Dr. Van Wagenen was elected President of the newly formed Harvey Cushing Society. During the initial meeting, the society met conjointly with the Boston Society of Neurology and Psychiatry the first evening and was welcomed by the president of the society, Dr. W. Jason Mixter.

One of the primary objectives in the minds of the group forming the Harvey Cushing Society was the setting up of the Brain Tumor Registry. This was accomplished at the second meeting in Louisville, Kentucky. It was the good fortune of the society that Dr. Cushing's associate in his study of intracranial tumors was available to set up the Brain Tumor Registry, and it was because of the leadership of

Dr. Louise Eisenhardt that this continued to function in such a fruitful manner after that time. [NOTE: for more information about the Cushing Brain Tumor Registry, visit the AANS Cyber Museum of Neurosurgery at http://www.neurosurgery.org/cybermuseum/tumor-registryhall/wahl.html.)

The next three meetings were held successively in St. Louis, New Haven, and Rochester, Minnesota, and the numerical membership level was raised to 50. Dr. Ernest Sachs was elected to Honorary Membership, the first to follow Dr. Cushing.

The society has met annually, with the exception of 1945; the meeting was cancelled that year because of the exigencies of World War II.

In 1937 there was much discussion of the unwieldy size of the growing organization, and a proposal was made that active members be retired after seven years but that they be allowed to attend meetings and dine as senior members. Dr. John Fulton, the president of the Harvey Cushing Society that year, seems to have changed the thinking of that proposal by the following statement: "Senior Members can, of course, dine, and that is all they would be good for. It would be better, to chloroform the Senior Members than to rally them. In short, I am not very much in sympathy with the idea of retiring people after seven years and then trying to keep them in good humor with dinners and rallies and invitations to speak now and again at meeting. Such an arrangement would, it seem to me, ruin the present sprit of the Society."

At the Memphis meeting in 1938, there was a discussion concerning the establishment of a Board of Neurological Surgery, and a report favoring the formation of such a board was submitted by Dr. Winchell McK. Craig.

In 1942 at the meeting in New York, the real expansion of the society began, following the acceptance of a committee report prepared at the previous meeting in Rochester, New York. Under the new bylaws of the society, all active members of the society were to be certified by the American Board of Neurological Surgery. The society was to be expanded into a neurosurgical organization of national scope and include representative members from related fields.

In 1943 the Harvey Cushing Society undertook the establishment of the *Journal of Neurosurgery*, appointed an editorial board under the chairmanship of Dr. Gilbert Horrax, and began publication in 1944 under the guiding hand of Dr. Eisenhardt as managing editor.

The Harvey Cushing Society grew phenomenally from the mid 1950s as more neurosurgeons were trained and became qualified. As they passed their American Board of Neurological Surgery examinations, most of them were proposed for membership in the Harvey Cushing Society and were elected to membership.

On advice of legal counsel, the Harvey Cushing Society became incorporated on June 6, 1956. New bylaws for conducting society business were adopted at the meeting of the society in April 1960.

At the Memphis meeting in 1938, there was a discussion concerning the establishment of a Board of Neurological Surgery...

Beginning a cherished tradition of the society in 1959, Dr. Cushing's nephew, Dr. E. H. Cushing, presented the society with the "Cushing cigarette box," to be inscribed with the name of each president and presented to each succeeding president upon assuming office. The box was originally given to Dr. Cushing by the surgical staff at Peter Bent

Brigham Hospital on April 14, 1931, commemorating Dr. Cushing's 2,000[th] intracranial tumor operation.

In 1961 a replica of the original was made, to be passed on to the presidents; the original is now housed in the Cushing Historical Library at the Yale Medical School. (Historical note: Yale gave the original and replica to the Archives of the American Association of Neurological Surgeons in 1985.)

On advice of legal counsel, the Harvey Cushing Society became incorporated on June 6, 1956.

Anticipating further growth, the Board of Directors of the Harvey Cushing Society began exploring, during the early 1960s, ways in which the society would best serve the interests of its membership. Looking over the correspondence of the secretaries of the society, it was evident that the Harvey Cushing Society also felt an obligation to represent all neurosurgeons in North America through continued education, representation on other national bodies, and representation to the national government.

At the 1962 meeting, Dr. H. S. Svien had the following comments:

> *"During the last several years I have occasionally had some misgivings and doubts as to whether or not The Harvey Cushing Society is fulfilling its obligations to its members. These misgivings and doubts can be pretty well summarized by asking the question, should neurosurgery in this country have an official spokesman: if so, who? Should The Harvey Cushing Society not be a bit more imaginative, a bit more aggressive, and provide a bit more in the way of leadership? There are many areas and problems which directly involve neurosurgery and neurosurgeons in this country*

*in which I think the Harvey Cushing Society should interest itself
and serve as an official spokesman."*

He then mentioned some of those areas and problems: television
programs (that was in the days of Dr. Ben Casey)—what the Harvey
Cushing Society should do if neurosurgeons or neurosurgery were
belittled; fee schedules—whether insurance companies should consult
more closely with neurosurgeons on that matter; professional box-
ing—is neurosurgery (and the Harvey Cushing Society) derelict in
its obligations to the public to expose the serious injuries inherent in
that sport?; Pantopaque—should the Harvey Cushing Society appoint
a committee to evaluate that agent and the complications of its use?;
and the training of foreign students—should the Harvey Cushing
Society see that those students are trained in their own countries since
the AMA had decided that they should not be training in hospitals in
the United States?

Dr. Svien continued,

> *"There are many, many other similar problems, which I think The
> Harvey Cushing Society could rightfully enter into. I think that
> the Board of Directors must ask themselves whether it is sufficient
> for The Harvey Cushing Society to simply present an annual
> program each year and to let it go at that. I suggest that there are
> many areas in which some leadership is needed and that the logi-
> cal organization to lead is The Harvey Cushing Society."*

Not mentioned in those minutes nor in the correspondence between
officers of the Harvey Cushing Society was an episode that sparked
profound change in the action of the Board of Directors: A president
of one of the other neurosurgical societies received an inquiry from
a federal agency asking that society, as the national representative
of neurosurgery, to make an appointment to the agency's board.

After some delay and a good deal of soul-searching, the president of that society responded that, in spite of the impressive titles of each of our national societies, he did not think his society represented neurosurgery nationally, and did not know which one did represent neurosurgery, if any one did.

That episode brought into action a number of moves by the Harvey Cushing Society to clarify the issue. Committees were established, and physicians with background skills and knowledge who would represent various segments of neurosurgery were appointed. The members of those committees worked long and hard, often at their own expense, to explore ways in which neurosurgery could be more effective as a specialty in North America, not only for its own interests, but for the more effective care of patients, and for a harmonious relationship with other national and regional societies.

The Harvey Cushing Society Annual Meeting, April 1956, Honolulu, Hawaii

Hence it was the presidents and secretaries of the five neurosurgical societies in North America, invited by the president of the Harvey Cushing Society, met several times to delineate objectives for neurosurgery and to seek ways to achieve those objectives.

A Mission and Structure Committee (originally called a liaison committee) came into being under the leadership of Dr. James Gay; its detailed reports were of immense help to the Board of Directors of the Harvey Cushing Society in eventually bringing about, under the leadership of President Frank Mayfield (with his April 12, 1965, proclamation), the unification of neurosurgery in North America. The changing of the name from the Harvey Cushing Society to the American Association of Neurological Surgeons (founded in 1931 as the Harvey Cushing Society) was a part of the process of making the AANS the spokesman for neurosurgery; the other major part was the ensuring of broad representation by putting on its Board of Directors physicians from all five neurosurgical societies in North America.

Dr. Louise Eisenhardt presented the first Cushing Oration, April 1965 in New York City, New York. With Dr. Eisenhardt are the Harvey Cushing Society officers, Dr. Eben Alexander (Secretary), Dr. Benjamin Whitcomb (Treasurer), Dr. Frank Mayfield (President), Dr. Eisenhardt, Dr. Edwin Boldrey (Vice President), and Dr. Francis Murphey (President-Elect).

HARVEY CUSHING SOCIETY
to
AMERICAN ASSOCIATION
of
NEUROLOGICAL
SURGEONS

THE YEARS OF GROWTH AND REFINEMENT

FRANK H. MAYFIELD, MD

Reminiscences

Reprinted from *History of the American Association of Neurological Surgeons founded in 1931 as the Harvey Cushing Society, 1931–1981*

THE INVITATION TO REMINISCE ABOUT PEOPLE and events leading up to and resulting in conversion of the Harvey Cushing Society to the American Association of Neurological Surgeons tempts me to take a nostalgic tour, year by year, of intimate friendships and delightful associations. Actually, however, there are only a few periods in which my recollections might enhance the historic record.

In the course of human events, judgments arrived at and decisions made cannot be isolated from one's perception at the time; history determines their merit. Hence, a brief review of my association with the Harvey Cushing Society seems appropriate in order to set the stage for my thoughts now.

The founding of the Harvey Cushing Society in 1931 and my graduation from medical school that year were unrelated events. Within two years, however, the new society began to influence my professional career. This influence increased sporadically over the years and eventually reached and has retained a dominant role in my life.

I was first aware of the existence of the Harvey Cushing Society in 1932 when one of my teachers, Dr. James G. Lyerly, was accepted into membership. In 1935 I accepted an invitation to join Dr. R. Glen Spurling on the faculty of the University of Louisville. Dr. Spurling was a founder of the society and a very active member of its governing board. Through this association I soon came to know all of the founders and many of the members of this exciting new organization.

My sense of exhilaration and anticipation was high when I joined six other young neurosurgeons (Evans, Braden, Echols, Raaf, Keith,

Murphey) as guests at the Memphis meeting of the "Cushing" in 1938.
Each of us had been led to believe by our sponsors that we would be
elected to membership that year. I will never forget the sense of frus-
tration and bitterness that engulfed me when I was informed, along
with the others, that the society had changed course and that none of
the seven was to be elected.

In anger, augmented by whiskey, the seven of us adjourned to our
rooms at the Peabody Hotel and organized the American Academy
of Neurological Surgery. This was not a noble beginning for what has
been an honored society, but it is a fact.

Unfortunately, the group closed its membership without recogniz-
ing that we were doing to others that which had been done to us.
Later, the Neurosurgical Society of America and then the Congress
of Neurological Surgeons were organized.

The desire by one for recognition and acceptance by his peers is a consuming human emotion. One wonders what course the specialty of
neurological surgery might have taken if the Society of Neurological
Surgeons or the Harvey Cushing Society or any of the other organizations had noted and responded appropriately to this obvious need.

I was pleased to be elected to membership in the Harvey Cushing
Society in 1941, but the experience was far less meaningful then than
it would have been to me in 1938.

My first official assignment as a member of the Harvey Cushing Society was to serve as a member of a committee to propose a method of
dealing with the foregoing problem, namely, how to make room for a
large group of oncoming people. The American Board of Neurological
Surgery had given its first examination in 1940. The Harvey Cushing Society then decided to use board certification as the standard
for qualification for admission to membership. The members of the
society were unwilling at that time to create provisional memberships

for those who were awaiting certification or who were in training. The organization was, therefore, not prepared to deal with the large numbers of people whose careers were interrupted by World War II and who returned shortly thereafter to resume training or begin careers as practitioners and teachers.

During the war and in the postwar period, I attended meetings of the Harvey Cushing Society regularly. I profited greatly from the learning experience and from the pleasant and stimulating associations. On the other hand, I took no significant part in the governance of the society. I did not attend the meeting of the society at which I was named president-elect and was most pleasantly surprised when I received a telegram from the secretary, Dr. Eben Alexander, advising me of this.

The federal program developed by President Lyndon Johnson to deal with the problems of heart, cancer, and stroke had just been approved.

The educational and social experiences derived from membership in the Harvey Cushing Society were consuming, but I continued to be concerned by its failure to deal with what I thought was an important problem. The post of president-elect, with the assurance that I would become president, appeared to me to provide the opportunity to address this issue.

The idea of using the Harvey Cushing Society as the vehicle for developing an organization to represent the neurosurgeons of the United States and Canada is mine, perhaps. The decision to take that course, and the monumental task of effecting the transition, involved so many dedicated people that I am hesitant to name any lest failure to identify one might appear to be lack of appreciation. The record, however requires that I do speak of some.

Francis Murphey had been named president-elect, and I knew that he recognized the problem. He agreed to support the concept of using the Cushing Society as a vehicle and to devote his administration to the transition if I could win the approval of the governing board of the Harvey Cushing Society for this idea.

Approval of the other national neurosurgical societies was, of course, essential for the concept to succeed. Discussions with the officers of the Society of Neurological Surgeons and of the American Academy of Neurological Surgery resulted in their approval for broadening the scope of the Harvey Cushing Society. I was not a member of the Neurosurgical Society of America, but several members of that organization, especially Bill Meacham and Collie MacCarty, agreed to present the idea to that association, and this group also approved.

The first opportunity to present the idea to the Board of Directors of the Harvey Cushing Society was at its annual meeting in New York in 1965. Eben Alexander, the secretary of the society, was in complete agreement and was most influential in helping me persuade the Board of Directors that the Harvey Cushing Society should indeed become the representative organization for all neurosurgeons in the United States and Canada. With few exceptions, the members of the board recognized the importance of the issue as it related to young neurosurgeons. Some were reluctant, for nostalgic reasons, to see the character of the organization change.

The federal program developed by President Lyndon Johnson to deal with the problems of heart, cancer, and stroke had just been approved. I presented to the board correspondence with Dr. Michael DeBakey, the president's medical representative for that program, and with Dr. John Sterling Meyer, who had been chosen by Dr. DeBakey to deal with the stroke section program. This correspondence left no doubt that the federal government and the major medical organizations such as the AMA could not identify any neurosurgical organization that was capable of serving as the spokesman for neurosurgeons. The board then authorized me to make the announcement that the Harvey Cushing Society would assume the responsibility as spokesman for neurosurgeons in the United States.

It had been suggested that the Congress of Neurological Surgeons, especially some past officers, might be less than enthusiastic about the idea. This proved not to be true. I called Gordon Van Den Noort and Bill Mosberg, president and president-elect of the Congress at that time, I believe, who were in attendance. These gentlemen agreed with the principle and agreed to undertake to persuade their colleagues to accept the idea. Dr. Francis Murphey, upon whose able shoulders the transition was to fall, assures me that their support was continuing during this period.

The Presidential Address that I had brought to New York then had to be rewritten. I will always be indebted to Dorothy Ayer, Dr. Eben Alexander's secretary, for rewriting and editing the Address known as "A Proclamation." It took her most of the night in order to get it done.

Before making the announcement that the Harvey Cushing Society would assume the new role, I thought it appropriate to interview as many past presidents and charter members as possible. Without exception, they agreed to support the proposal. Dr. Glen Spurling endorsed the idea; he thanked me for calling him that night. He did express the hope that it would not be necessary to change the name. All of the founders and many of the original members had this same nostalgic feeling.

There were a number of other momentous events taking place at that annual meeting that I would like to refer to. Among these events was a major change in the *Journal of Neurosurgery*. Dr. Louise Eisenhardt had organized the *Journal* and had been its editor from the beginning.

Her health made it difficult for her to keep up with the workload, and the decision had been made to offer the post to Dr. Henry Heyl. Dr. Bronson Ray, at my request, made several personal visits to Dr. Eisenhardt and succeeded in convincing her of the wisdom of this decision. The society had in the meantime decided to establish a lectureship to be known as the Cushing Oration, and the Board of Directors were unanimous in demanding that Dr. Eisenhardt be the first Cushing Orator.

Ben and Betty Whitcomb brought Dr. Eisenhardt to New York and served as her ubiquitous hosts. Dr. Eisenhardt had not felt well enough to prepare a formal address; instead, she elected to bring her diary with her (commonly known as the little black book) and reminisced from it. For those who had known Dr. Eisenhardt and Dr. Cushing, it was a moving moment. There were few dry eyes in the audience.

One last acknowledgment that I would like to make has to do with the scientific program of the society. With the broadening of the mission of the society, it seemed appropriate to modify to some extent the scientific programs. Dr. Frank Nulsen was the chairman of the Program Committee and initiated the series of Breakfast Seminars which have become popular over the years. It was his vision, I think, that created the seed from which the remarkable programs that we now have evolved.

Finally, let me say that I have watched with interest, approval, and some pride the evolution of the American Association of Neurological Surgeons. The mild controversies which have occurred from time to time and which led to reorganization of the constitution recently have, I think, strengthened the organization rather than weakened it. Someone has said that democracy should preserve for individuals the right to choose their leaders, but that if democracy is to function well and survive, the leaders elected should be aristocrats. No constitution should be cast in stone; the strength of an organization is in the confidence of its members.

THE HARVEY CUSHING
SOCIETY

THIRTY-THIRD ANNUAL MEETING
THE AMERICANA HOTEL
NEW YORK, NEW YORK
APRIL 11-15, 1965

THE AMERICAN ASSOCIATION
OF NEUROLOGICAL SURGEONS
founded in 1931 as
The Harvey Cushing Society

THIRTY-SIXTH ANNUAL MEETING
THE CONRAD HILTON HOTEL
CHICAGO, ILLINOIS
APRIL 7-11, 1968

THE HARVEY CUSHING SOCIETY
THE AMERICAN ASSOCIATION OF NEUROLOGICAL SURGEONS

THIRTY-FIFTH ANNUAL MEETING
THE SAN FRANCISCO-HILTON
SAN FRANCISCO, CALIFORNIA

APRIL 16-20, 1967

 SAN FRANCISCO
EVERYBODY'S FAVORITE CITY

HISTORY OF
the AMERICAN ASSOCIATION
of NEUROLOGICAL
SURGEONS

1965–1980

WILLIAM F. MEACHAM, MD

Reprinted from *History of the American Association of Neurological Surgeons founded in 1931 as The Harvey Cushing Society, 1931–1981*

THE ADDRESS OF DR. FRANK MAYFIELD, PRESIDENT of the Harvey Cushing Society in 1965 at New York City, had a profound effect on organized neurosurgery. His address, titled "A Proclamation," stated that the Harvey Cushing Society should be recognized as the official voice for neurosurgery in the United States, and suggested that each national society consider this and, if feasible, cooperate in the establishment of this society as the official neurosurgical organization.

Accordingly, ad hoc committees were appointed to (a) facilitate appropriate broad representation on the Board of Directors, (b) study and propose changes in the constitution in consonance with the official stature of the society, and (c) suggest altering or changing the name of the society to more effectively indicate its official position.

The dedicated industriousness of the ad hoc committees was apparent by the time of the 1966 meeting in St. Louis. Constitutional changes approved changing the name to the Harvey Cushing Society Inc. (the American Association of Neurological Surgeons). The constituency of the Board of Directors was altered to include the president, vice president, president-elect, secretary, treasurer, chairman of the Membership Committee, the two immediate past presidents, and a representative each from the Society of Neurological Surgeons, the American Academy of Neurological Surgery, the Neurosurgical Society of America, and the Congress of Neurological Surgeons. All members of the Board of Directors were required to be members of the Harvey Cushing Society, and the term of appointment was for three years. Other details relating to the *Journal of Neurosurgery*, the American Board of Neurological Surgery, and the Liaison Committee were considered. The scientific programs were continued with

in other areas was acknowledged by the entire membership. The editorial responsibilities remained with Dr. Henry Heyl and the Editorial Board, and the printing of the *Journal* was changed from the Banta Company in Chicago to the Dartmouth Printing Company in Hanover, New Hampshire. The Williams and Wilkins Company of Baltimore remained responsible for advertising, subscriptions, and accounting.

A new group, the Joint Socio-Economics Committee, composed of members from the AANS and the Congress of Neurological Surgeons, was formed, and plans for several subcommittees were formulated. This group was destined to have great influence in the ensuing years in the development of concepts relating to terminology, peer review, malpractice problems, and state and regional advisory committees. [Historical note: This group is now call the Council of State Neurosurgical Societies.]

By 1974, the Committee on Education under the chairmanship of Dr. Robert King had made commendable progress in all phases of its activity. Eight subcommittees were deeply involved in the phases of education pertinent to neurosurgery and its impact on the government and the public. Undergraduate, graduate, and continuing education problems remain the concern of this group.

The Professional Liability Committee also committed itself to continued work to reconcile the national problem of medical liability in malpractice lawsuits. The efforts of Dr. William Hunt and his committee rendered a meaningful service to the organization.

By the time of the St. Louis (1974) meeting, the final organization of the Joint Socio-Economics Committee had materialized and all subcommittee assignments made, and, more important, all state and local groups had been formed under four topographical areas.

The death of Dr. Henry Heyl in March 1975 was the terminus of a decade of dedicated work as the editor of our *Journal*. All neurosurgeons shared in his loss. His replacement by Dr. Henry Schwartz was a blessing approved by all.

> *The death of Dr. Henry Heyl in March 1975 was the terminus of a decade of dedicated work as the editor of our* Journal.

Drs. Gerard Guiot, Keiji Sano, Gosta Norlen, and Hugo Krayenbuhl were elected to honorary membership.

The San Francisco meeting (1976) and the Toronto meeting (1977) were characterized by exceptionally fine scientific programs and other educational activities, along with superb social and recreational activities. One important business item concerned the termination of our long-term association with Mr. Michael O'Connor and the Williams and Wilkins Company and the selection (after thorough research) of Mr. Carl Hauber to be the executive director with the National Office, to be located in Chicago. The Board of Directors also established an award to be known as the Harvey Cushing Medal to be given to a member for distinguished and meritorious service.

By 1978 (New Orleans), the bylaws were amended to allow for nine classes of membership, namely: Active, Active (Foreign), Associate, Lifetime, Senior, Corresponding, Honorary, Candidate, and Inactive.

The business meetings of 1976, 1977, and 1978 revealed a segment of concern among many of the members that the society's government was not appropriately democratic, and several attempts to change the method of selection of the directors were made. Finally, it was approved that four members-at-large would be elected, one from each of the four regional districts, in addition to the officers, the two past presidents, and a representative from each of the five national societies. The Board of Directors was authorized to act as a nominating committee for the new officers with nominations from the floor being allowed.

By 1978, it seemed, therefore, that the organization had "arrived" as national spokesman for our specialty. During the following two years, development of the association's activities, scientific programs, educational activities, relationship with other organizations, and the continued improvement in our journal were all manifest. It has become clear that the association will face many exciting challenges in the future.

American
Association of
Neurological
Surgeons

and the American Association of Neurosurgeons

2007 AANS ANNUAL MEETING

Program Guide

CELEBRATING AANS' DIAMOND JUBILEE

WASHINGTON, DC   APRIL 14–19, 2007

HISTORY *in the* MAKING

AANS CELEBRATES ITS DIAMOND JUBILEE

DONALD O. QUEST, MD

THE 75ᵀᴴ ANNIVERSARY OF THE FOUNDING of the organization that has become the American Association of Neurological Surgeons (AANS) is an opportune time to reflect on the evolution of the field of neurological surgery as well as the evolution of the association.

The Harvey Cushing Society, named for the founder of American neurosurgery and one of the world's great neurosurgeons, was organized as a club by a small number of like-minded surgeons. These valiant and indomitable individuals came together to develop a new specialty of medicine in the face of inhospitable, nearly insurmountable odds. None of them could envision the astonishing developments in medicine that would change neurosurgery from a desperate undertaking to one that provides patients with definitive cures or long-lasting and welcome palliation. In 1931 such advances as contemporary understanding of molecular biology and genetics, spine instrumentation, implantable device technology, innovative imaging modalities, modern pharmaceuticals, and chemotherapy were simply unimaginable.

Along with the growth of neurosurgery as a specialty, the AANS has flourished since its inception 75 years ago and has developed into a body which encompasses the full spectrum of neurological surgery and touches on every aspect of the field.

The AANS is the organization that speaks for all of neurosurgery. It has encouraged the development of all the subspecialty groups within the field and maintains them under its aegis, unifying all aspects of the specialty. It fosters collegial relationships with other professional organizations within neurological surgery, with the house of surgery in general—and indeed with all of medicine. Communication and cooperation are essential among all these various entities and are the foundation on which the AANS relies when advocating on behalf of neurosurgery to widely diverse audiences —the public, the medical community in general, the government, the media, and third party payers.

Devotion to patients is the mainspring of the neurosurgical profession. The AANS therefore is devoted to advancing the specialty in order to promote the highest quality of patient care. The means for fulfilling this goal are multifaceted, refined, and often complex.

Neurosurgeons are recognized as the preeminent providers of quality care to patients with surgical disorders that affect the entire nervous system. Among the many reasons underlying achievement of this esteem are the intensive training and ongoing education required. The AANS helps meet these stringent requisites by providing a multitude of educational opportunities.

Among these opportunities are AANS-produced Web-based offerings, publications, and regional meetings designed to fulfill Maintenance of Certification requirements recently developed by the American Board of Neurological Surgery. An Internet database system is under development to provide members with a sophisticated and comprehensive vehicle for operative data collection, practice assessment, and continuing medical education. Online compilation of continuing medical educational credits is provided for all members and, in conjunction with the Society of Neurological Surgeons, Internet-based learning modules have been developed to augment resident and member education.

The AANS is its members' principal resource for professional interaction regarding the ever-expanding scope of neurosurgical care, new technologies, and treatments of neurological disorders. The AANS' numerous meetings and periodicals—the *Bulletin*, the *Journal of Neurosurgery*, the *Journal of Neurosurgery: Spine*, the *Journal of Neurosurgery: Pediatrics*, and *Neurosurgical Focus*—and various Internet-based assets all provide practice information and educational resources to members.

Research is the key to the future of neurological surgery, an endeavor the AANS officially recognized through the establishment of the

Neurosurgery Research and Education Foundation (NREF) in 1981. The NREF has since grown dramatically in its ability to provide financial support to young neurosurgical investigators, helping them to develop their careers in clinical and basic research.

Continuous outreach to the international community has increased interaction between the AANS and various international neurosurgical societies, including the World Federation of Neurosurgical Societies. The AANS Annual Meeting is truly an international event with a multitude of attendees from around the globe as well as many scientific offerings presented by international members.

The AANS membership is representative of the entire scope of neurosurgery with major efforts to enhance the role of young neurosurgeons, foster the participation of resident members, and encourage medical student involvement in AANS activities, especially the annual meeting. Diversification of the neurosurgical workforce is a major goal. Motivating more women to enter the field is among expanded efforts to ensure that the best and brightest medical students enter neurosurgery.

The AANS has turned its attention to professional liability in answer to pressures originating within a greater part of society. One of the critical issues in recent years is the unfavorable professional liability climate and its increasing costs and burdens that affect all neurosurgeons. The AANS has responded in part through expansion of its Professional Conduct Program, which was established in 1982. The program endeavors to ensure that the Rules for Neurosurgical Medical/Legal Expert Opinion and the Code of Ethics promulgated by the AANS are adhered to, and that honest, informed, and unbiased testimony is provided during legal proceedings.

The AANS has worked for professional liability reform through the Washington Committee. Formed in 1975 in recognition that interaction with the federal government would need to become a major activity of the AANS, this committee spearheads neurosurgery's advocacy not only for professional liability reform but also regarding physician payment, quality improvement, and patient safety initiatives that require careful analysis coupled with vigorous and knowledgeable advocacy. A new political action committee for neurosurgery also has been formed in order to further the legislative goals of neurosurgery and ensure the best care for patients.

An example of how the many facets of the AANS work together to incorporate new technologies and advance the profession can be seen within stereotactic radiosurgery (SRS), a therapy that was unimaginable in 1931. During its 75th year, the AANS and appropriate stakeholders agreed on a contemporary, comprehensive definition of SRS. The definition recognizes SRS as a distinct discipline that utilizes externally generated ionizing radiation to inactivate or eradicate defined targets in the head and spine non-invasively. It also calls for performance of SRS by a multidisciplinary team to ensure quality patient care. The AANS published the definition as a position statement and spearheaded advocacy efforts to encourage Medicare and third party payers to adopt it. The AANS further supports neurosurgeons subspecializing in SRS through its support of the AANS/CNS Section on Stereotactic and Functional Neurosurgery and through the many educational opportunities the AANS offers.

Examples such as this suggest that when today's neurosurgeons ask questions which our progeny 75 years hence might find rudimentary, simplistic, and naive, such as where innovations in biomechanical prostheses or in stem cell research might lead us, we can feel confident that whatever transpires, the AANS will adapt appropriately to lead neurosurgery in incorporating advances and best practices that achieve quality patient care.

This ability to adapt is rooted not only in a clear idea of the AANS mission and vision, but also in the organization's infrastructure. The democratically elected AANS Board of Directors represents the broad spectrum of neurosurgical practice. Directors are assigned divisions for which they are responsible, reflecting the organization's complexity: Operations & Planning, Communications, Practice, Education, and Science. In addition, more than 400 neurosurgeons volunteer at the committee level, helping to ensure that issues important to their colleagues, wherever they may practice, are addressed.

The AANS executive office and the Washington office are staffed by dedicated and knowledgeable professionals who provide the infrastructure for the many complex activities of the organization and help guide the organization in a business-like fashion.

Leadership and staff together have developed broad-based revenue sources to fund the ever-enlarging matrix of AANS activities so that member benefits can be enhanced without increasing individual members' financial burden. Revenue enhancement has been achieved through the annual meeting, courses, and publication revenues, along with corporate donations. The strong financial position that the AANS maintains constitutes a firm position from which the AANS can achieve its vision, embodied in its host of initiatives.

"Prediction is very difficult, especially about the future," says an aphorism attributed to Nobel laureate physicist Niels Bohr (although it sounds more like an observation of "baseball philosopher" Yogi Berra). This maxim certainly applies to neurosurgery and to the AANS. Exciting possibilities lie just ahead, and the capacity of the AANS to adapt and to lead under changing and challenging circumstances bodes well for neurosurgery's future. The advent of nanotechnology, only an inchoate spark at the time of the AANS' 50th anniversary, now has ignited great excitement in the biological sciences because of its fabulous potential to revolutionize diagnostic and therapeutic modalities. Fantastic advances in diagnostic sensitivity and specificity appear possible along with highly precise and focused medical intervention at the molecular level for curing disease and repairing tissue. Terminology such as nanoparticles, nanotubes, nanowires, quantum dots, fullerenes, femtosecond lasers, and concepts such as microelectromechanical systems, molecular manufacturing, and quantum computers have the ring of science fiction in the present day but very likely will be part of the neurosurgical lexicon at the time of the AANS' 100th anniversary.

The legacy of neurosurgery's founders provides inspiration and guidance, illuminating the path as the specialty of neurosurgery faces the future with dedication and a creative spirit. This Diamond Jubilee year is one of celebration for the venerable ideals of the AANS founders which have remained unchanged since the inception of the organization. The unity, vigor, purposefulness, productivity, and creativity of the AANS will continue to grow as the future unfolds.

Journal of
Neurosurgery

JANUARY 1944

Journal of Neurosurgery

JANUARY 1974 Volume 40, Number 1

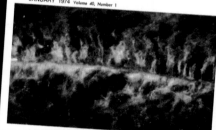

Journal of Neurosurgery

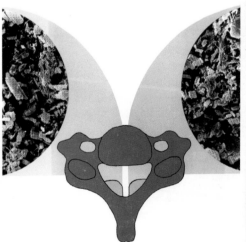

JANUARY 1984 Volume 60, Number 1

HISTORY OF
the JOURNAL *of*
NEUROSURGERY

JOHN A. JANE SR., MD, PHD, EDITOR

IN 1981, AN ANNIVERSARY VOLUME COMMEMORATING the 50th year of the Harvey Cushing Society/AANS was published. The early and later years of the *Journal of Neurosurgery (JNS)* were described by Paul Bucy and Henry Schwartz, respectively. Significant changes have quite understandably taken place in the last 25 years, and recounting these changes and the reasons that underlay their implementation was deemed worthwhile. In 1994, in the 50th Anniversary issue of the *JNS*, Edward R. Laws analyzed the history and influence of the publication up to that time, using the words of Harvey Cushing as his text.

A résumé of the earlier years will help delineate the aspects of the *JNS* that have not changed and those that have. The *JNS* began publication in 1944 with Louise Eisenhardt as editor and Gilbert Horrax as chairman of an Editorial Board that consisted of five members. The first volume of the *JNS* contained six issues. Each article was reviewed by every member of the board, a mechanism that has been modified but not abandoned. A unique characteristic of the present-day Editorial Board is that each reviewer independently reads the article. The reviews are done successively with the previous reviewers' comments available to them. The manuscript is sent to the next reviewer, then to the chairman, and finally to the editor for a final decision. A gradual increase in the size of the Editorial Board reflecting the increase of submissions began slowly in 1984 when it consisted of seven members, including myself. In the 1990s, 12 members handled the reviews, but with the advent of *Neurosurgical Focus* in 1997 under the direction of Martin Weiss and an organizational change of two chairmen instead of one, 14 members were appointed. The *Journal of Neurosurgery (JNS): Spine* began publication in 1999, and the *Journal of Neurosurgery (JNS): Pediatrics* became the official journal of the American Society of Pediatric Neurosurgeons in 2004.

Over the years, a gradual increase reflecting growth in the number of neurosurgeons and the expanding horizon of the field was reflected in the current complement of 48 issues consisting of 12 each of the *JNS*, the *JNS: Spine*, the *JNS: Pediatrics*, and *Neurosurgical Focus*. All together, they are now referred to as the JNS Publishing Group.

The selection of the editor and the Editorial Board has changed, and the process may be of interest, reflecting as it does, a general trend towards democracy, probably applauded by many but perhaps not all neurosurgeons.

The first editor, Louise Eisenhardt, and the five-member Editorial Board were chosen by John Fulton, who was considered the founder of the *JNS*. Alfonso Asenjo was closely involved with the process. During the next 20 years, the Editorial Board members were chosen by the Editorial Board itself and remained at five to six members. In 1965, Dr. Eisenhardt was no longer able to continue her duties, and it became necessary to appoint a new editor. Henry Schwartz, who believed that Paul Bucy had selected him for the board, conferred with Eben Alexander. In Dr. Schwartz's own words, in a taxi ride to the Chicago airport, they decided that Henry Heyl should be the next editor. Dr. Schwartz told me at the time of our conversation on September 8, 1997, not to make this public as it seemed to him to be somewhat "high-handed." The passage of time and the innate interest of the story have persuaded me to reveal this. Dr. Heyl remained editor until his death in 1975. Dr. Schwartz further told me that he felt that Charles Drake was instrumental in his appointment as editor. Henry Schwartz's tenure lasted until 1985 when William Collins took over. This somewhat arbitrary but effective decision making characterized the early years of the *JNS*.

In a recent conversation, Dr. Collins described his selection and those of the Editorial Board members as basically Dr. Schwartz's decision, although in Dr. Collins' case, he remembers that an election was actually held.

Dr. Collins began the process of increasing the number of members of the board while maintaining the successive, not simultaneous review process. He asked the advice of the Editorial Board as to new members. He decided to step down in 1990, and Thoralf Sundt Jr. was elected. Only former board members who were nominated by the Editorial Board or the Advisory were considered as candidates. The final selection was made by a vote of the then current Editorial Board.

In 1997 the Editorial Board approved our electronic journal, **Neurosurgical Focus.**

During the next three years, Dr. Sundt selected new Editorial Board members in consultation with the chairman of the Editorial Board, but without a vote being taken. After Dr. Sundt's death in September 1992, candidates were again solicited, and a final vote of the Editorial Board in October 1992 resulted in my selection as editor. The following changes have subsequently taken place. The Editorial Board members are now selected by a vote, the term varying from six to eight years, the last year spent as co-chairman of the board. The two co-chairmen review all the manuscripts before sending them on to the editor for a final judgment. Thus, the Editorial Board members review 200 to 600 papers per year and the co-chairmen close to 1,000. The dedication involved in this effort is impossible to overestimate in its importance to the *JNS* and the practice of neurosurgery.

In 1997 the Editorial Board approved our electronic journal, *Neuro-surgical Focus.* Martin Weiss led this initiative. *Neurosurgical Focus* has become a critical aspect of the JNS Publishing Group since it represents an ongoing trend in publishing. It has captured a worldwide audience with its up-to-date topic-oriented issues.

In 1998 the co-chairmanship of the Editorial Board had been established because of the increased workload, and at this time, two trends in neurosurgery became insistent and impossible for the *JNS* to ignore. They were as follows.

Pediatric neurosurgeons had since the time of Ingraham and Matson considered their work to be distinct. Their rallying cry was children were not simply little adults. The formation of societies dedicated to the surgery of infants and children was inevitable. One of these societies, the American Association of Pediatric Neurosurgery, began the journal *Pediatric Neurosurgery* and a separate certifying board with their own qualifications and examinations. There was, to say the least, considerable agitation in neurosurgery and at the American Board of Neurological Surgery, in particular. There was perceived to be a serious threat that pediatric neurosurgery might secede from the main body of neurosurgery, an event not as cosmic as our Civil War, but to the welfare of neurosurgery, just as damaging.

The second similar movement was taking place among spine surgeons, always a major part of our clinical practice. Rapid and dramatic changes in the care of spine patients, the increasing use of instrumentation, the recognition of the AANS leadership, led by David Kelly, that residents in training had to adapt to the new reality, gave the individuals involved a sense of being separate. This, in turn, suggested that perhaps joining with orthopedic surgeons in a new specialty called spine surgery was the inevitable future.

Two answers to these separatist movements were possible. One, akin to *Brown v. the Board of Education*, was to say separate but equal was unworkable and both groups should be allowed to secede. The other solution, akin to *Plessy v. Ferguson*, was to take the position that these two areas could indeed live as separate but equal. One way to empower both was to give them their own journal, hence was born the *JNS: Spine* and the *JNS: Pediatrics*. Their birth was an effort to keep neurosurgery together. The obvious expertise and sensational development that each had already undergone made them, in a real sense, separate but equal. This separation is further expressed in different journals with independent boards, each journal being published on a monthly basis. At the present time, there remains overlap so that they are not entirely separate. For example, spine surgeons may help with occasional pediatric problems, and pediatric surgeons often add sophistication to the management of, for example, pediatric problems in patients who are now adults. Moreover, the three boards while meeting separately have unequivocally decided to meet together at the AANS annual meetings. I am persuaded that the formation of these three journals was important in keeping neurosurgery together in this time which we all acknowledge as one of unique peril to our beloved specialty.

Further separation is not now being contemplated. Functional, stereotactic, oncology, pain, peripheral nerve, socioeconomic issues, and vascular topics all fit quite well in the present journal. Article-based publication is being considered, and our new managing editor, Adrienne Lea, will be closely involved in this process. She follows Jean Lawe, Keller Kaufman-Fox, and Barbara Meyers, all of whom have made major contributions. Margie Shreve, who began with Thoralf Sundt, remains essential to the well-being of the *JNS* and is familiar with every contributor. The editorial staff and the managers, Jo Ann Eliason, Gillian Shasby, Susan McDonald, Susan Lanterman, and Evelyn Kessler take pride in their commitment to maintaining the highest standards in redaction and production.

To paraphrase Thomas Jefferson, the changes that have taken place at the *JNS* have been done for us and for the benefit of those who come after us. I hope that its influence on their virtue, freedom, fame, and fortune will be salutory and permanent.

For a list of the JNS chairs, please refer to Pages 121–123.

Journal of Neurosurgery

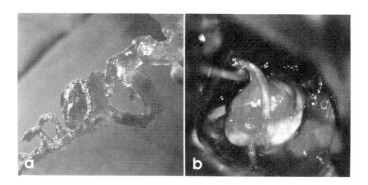

American Association of Neurological Surgeons

JANUARY 2004 Volume 100, Number 1

WWW.THEJNS-NET.ORG

Celebrating
NREF
25 Years

1981- 2006

Neurosurgery
Research
and
Education
Foundation
(NREF)

Thank you
for
your support!
www.AANS.org

Neurosurgical Research and *and* Education Foundation (NREF)

Then . . . Now . . . Future— Celebrating 25 Years of Research

MARTIN H. WEISS, MD, FACS

To deny research the support it warrants is akin to eating next year's seed corn.—Unknown

Why was the NREF established?

ORIGINALLY KNOWN AS THE RESEARCH FOUNDATION of the American Association of Neurological Surgeons, the program was designed to stimulate and make possible a broader effort in basic neurological research through financial support to young neurosurgeons while they were undergoing refinement of their basic science techniques, methodology, and skills pertinent to neurobiology. Because federal funding for training purposes had become inadequate over the years, dropping a third from $12.3 million in 1973 to $8.9 million in 1980, support from private sources was urgently needed. The AANS Board of Directors determined that a separate research support division needed to be established, governed by an executive council, which included neurosurgeons, neuroscientists, and interested laypersons. The start-up costs of the Research Foundation were provided by the AANS until the endowment (it was determined that $2 million would be sufficient enough to start) was able to generate enough income to pay back the indebtedness to the AANS. A capital fundraising campaign was instituted with 100 percent of the pledges designated to the endowment; and all neurosurgeons and the neurosurgical community were asked for support, in addition to corporations, foundations, grateful patients, and interested private citizens.

The Research Foundation established two types of awards: the Research Fellowship (RF) and Young Clinician Investigator Award (YCI). The first two RF awards were bestowed in 1983; each was a $20,000 grant. The first two YCI Awards were given out in 1986 and were also $20,000 each.

What has it accomplished?

BETWEEN 1981 WHEN IT WAS ESTABLISHED AND the late 1990s, the Research Foundation's endowment had reached a market value of more than $4.6 million. To date, that endowment stands at $6.64 million.

Since the first grants were awarded in 1983, nearly $4.5 million has been allocated, supporting 113 investigations in all neurosurgical disciplines including: cerebrovascular, pain, pediatrics, spine, trauma, and tumors.

Other accomplishments, many of which are ongoing, include:

≫ Secured funding for special named lectures occurring annually at AANS annual meetings.

> 1. Richard C. Schneider Lecture
> 2. Ronald L. Bittner Lecture
> 3. Hunt-Wilson Lecture
> 4. Rhoton Family Lecture
> 5. Theodore Kurze Lecture

≫ Held first Annual Silent Auction in 1998 in conjunction with the AANS' Young Neurosurgeons Committee.

≫ Held first fundraising event, Ray Charles concert, in Chicago in conjunction with 2002 AANS Annual Meeting.

≫ Established formal memorial and tribute-giving program in 2003.

≫ Established NREF contributions appeal through the AANS membership dues billing in 2004.

≫ Established online giving opportunity through AANS Web site in 2004.

≫ Awarded most grants ever (13) in 2006.

Where is it headed in the future?

THE NEXT 25 YEARS ARE CRITICAL TO THE NREF. With the continued reduction in federal funding for neurosurgical research (NIH), the NREF is in a position of added importance and increased need for support to fund worthy, much-needed scientific investigations. Residents and young clinician investigators will look to the NREF for financial resources no longer available through government sources or through their own academic institutions.

The NREF will continue to fund as many high-quality research grants as it has funds to support. Added support will need to come to the NREF through Planned Giving/Estate Gifts as well as through annual and major gifts from AANS members and their families.

The NREF hopes to assist residents and young faculty members with their grant-writing skills through an annual breakfast seminar. The NREF will also continue to partner with other medical associations and subspecialty sections on research grants.

Finally, the NREF will continue its fundraising program, aiming to annually secure more support from the AANS membership, groups, corporations, and the general public through all of its appeals and numerous giving programs.

For a list of the Research Foundation and Neurosurgical Research and Education Foundation leaders and awardees, please refer to Page 123.

The AANS Board of Directors determined that a separate research support division needed to be established, governed by an executive council, which included neurosurgeons, neuroscientists, and interested laypersons.

AANS National Office building, 1984–2000, Park Ridge, Illinois

A NATIONAL OFFICE
for the
AMERICAN ASSOCIATION
of NEUROLOGICAL
SURGEONS

1978–2006

CHRIS ANN PHILIPS
AANS ARCHIVIST

AS EARLY AS 1968, THE AANS DISCUSSED THE need to have a "home office." In 1976 the AANS Board of Directors voted to establish a national office to shift financial and association management responsibilities from volunteer effort. After a lengthy search, Carl H. Hauber, JD, CAE was hired in 1977. The AANS National Headquarters' first location was at 625 North Michigan Avenue in Chicago, Illinois, and the workforce consisted of Hauber, a Kelly Girl (temporary help), and an IBM Selectric typewriter.

Initial efforts to centralize files and corporate materials were at times met with resistance from some members who were used to controlling aspects of member services. Eventually, things such as membership application processing, CME tracking, and section accounting practices were all managed by the AANS professional staff. An archive was established to protect corporate history as well as that of the specialty, and the "Leaders in Neuroscience" video interview series captured the memories and histories of many of the specialties leaders (For a list of the interviewees, please refer to Page 149).

The 1980s saw expansion of association management technology and opportunities to better serve neurosurgeons. In answer to the increasing workload and staffing needs, the AANS moved to Park Ridge, Illinois, in 1984. The Board of Directors approved funds to expand computer memory from 48M to 64M (current configurations are a gigabyte). The AANS annual meeting was evolving, requiring major formatting changes to its various publications. Staff worked with the Research Foundation (now called the Neurosurgical Research and Education Foundation) fundraising efforts and coordinated the grant application process. Much of the National Head and Spinal Cord Injury Prevention Program (later Think First) was managed by AANS. Staff worked with organizations such as the National Center for Health Statistics surveying member demographics (the basis for the current Neurosurgical Census). The original American Association of Neurosurgical Nurses was housed at the AANS national office and supported by staff. In an effort to better understand and coordinate the activities of the burgeoning committee structure, the board required an expanding reporting mechanism resulting in staff-prepared collections of information for board members to review that were in six-inch-thick binders. Working with the Washington office, staff coordinated efforts with the U.S. Postal Service to publish the Cushing Stamp in 1988, including an unveiling at the White House Rose Garden with President and Mrs. Reagan. By the end of the decade, fax was becoming the preferred communications vehicle for many offices, and staff collected fax numbers for more than 3,000 members for the annual membership directory.

Dr. Robert Ojemann talks with President and Mrs. Reagan and with Betsey Cushing Whitney at the Cushing Stamp Ceremony in Washington, DC, April 1988.

The efforts and systemization of the 1980s allowed for the AANS to support new growth areas in the next decade. When the Publications Committee published its first book in 1990, there was a need for the development of catalogs and distribution processes (For a bibliography of AANS publications, please refer to Page 142). AANS had an editorial staff, initially in Park Ridge and subsequently moved to Hanover, New Hampshire. In addition, a warehouse was purchased to house the book distribution center and the print shop facility. The Professional Development Program (now called Education and Practice Management) was initiated. Meeting management services were provided to outside organizations including the Congress of Neurological Surgeons (CNS), the Southern Neurosurgical Society, the World Federation of Neurosurgical Societies' International Congress, and the Latin American Congress, in addition to section meetings and the AANS annual meeting. The "AANS *Newsletter*" evolved into the "AANS *Bulletin*." In cooperation with the CNS, a joint Web site— Neurosurgery://On-Call—was established. Wang word processing was

AANS Executive Office building as of 2000, Rolling Meadows, Illinois

replaced with personal computers, and e-mail became the most common form of communication with members.

With Mr. Hauber's retirement in 1996, Robert E. Draba, PhD, was hired as the executive director. Dr. Draba gave the membership an opportunity to understand the uses of their dues with the development of the Annual Report to the Membership. The AANS was undergoing an office-wide data processing expansion in preparation for Y2K. A great deal of effort went into providing documentation of all materials AANS distributed about pedicle screws for federal court litigation. Increased activities of the Council of State Neurosurgical Societies meant expanding support to them. Dr. Draba left the AANS, and Dave Fellers became the executive director in 1999. The office building in Park Ridge was at capacity, and the search was underway to locate a new facility that would house both the office staff and warehouse.

To start the new century, AANS staff faced difficult challenges. Various adverse financial factors required cuts in the budget at the same time it was decided that dues would not be increased. The office was moved to Rolling Meadows, Illinois. Mr. Fellers left and was replaced by Thomas A. Marshall, promoted from within the organization, to executive director in late 2000.

Mr. Marshall initiated measures to bring the AANS back to fiscal stability. Innovative ideas and savvy computer programs allowed the AANS to provide good member service and expanded benefits. The AANS established its own Web site, AANS.org. New ventures to increase non-dues revenues were implemented. Successful educational programs were expanded, resulting in increased numbers of registrants at the annual meeting and Education and Practice Management courses. Opportunities to obtain the CME essential to the practice of good neurosurgery have been made available through online education and testing vehicles such as *Neurosurgical Focus*. The association's technological prowess allowed for the expansion of personalized online services and electronic delivery systems to replace many of the costly paper mailings for both members and exhibitors. Guidelines for Corporate Relations were established, allowing for ethical and fiscally responsible corporate support.

These and other efforts have been crucial in enabling the AANS to enter a "renaissance." This more balanced environment has attracted other neurosurgical organizations to work closely with the AANS through contract services including Web sites, both public and password protected, and in some cases, membership and meeting services. The AANS made a successful bid to manage the 2009 World Federation of Neurosurgical Societies meeting. Growth of services is vital to the well-being of the AANS staff and members.

Over the years, the relationship between leadership, members, and staff has been a choreography of styles from slam dancing to waltz. The AANS professional staff is confident in their firmly established ability to adapt to this choreography to manage the daily business of the association.

Journal of

Neurosurgery

JANUARY 1954

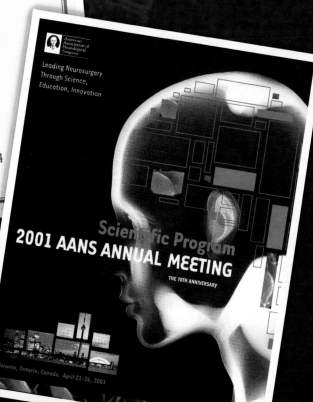

PEOPLE,
PLACES,
and PUBLICATIONS
in AANS HISTORY

Charter Members

THE CHARTER MEMBERS OF THE Harvey Cushing Society were selected in 1931, and they remained the nucleus of the society for many years, guiding its growth and development. The society they formed 75 years ago has changed in many ways, but it remains constant to the original objective of the promotion and advancement of the various fields of organic neurology.

Gilbert Anderson, MD
Paul C. Bucy, MD
W. Edward Chamberlain, MD
Leo M. Davidoff, MD
Louise Eisenhardt, MD
Temple Fay, MD
Edgar F. Fincher Jr., MD
John F. Fulton, PhD
W. James Gardner, MD
William J. German, MD
Franc D. Ingraham, MD
Franklin Jelsma, MD
Edgar A. Kahn, MD
Roland Klemme, MD
James G. Lyerly Sr., MD
Eric Oldberg, MD, PhD
Tracy J. Putnam, MD
Frederic Schreiber, MD
R. Eustace Semmes, MD
Merrill C. Sosman, MD
R. Glen Spurling, MD
Frank R. Teachenor, MD
William P. Van Wagenen, MD

Harvey Cushing Society—American Association of Neurological Surgeons Presidents and Annual Meeting

The annual meeting has a personality that is dependent on not only the president of the organization but the meeting location, speakers, and number of potential attendees. This section documents in part these elements and the growth of the organization.

William P. Van Wagenen, MD
1932–1933
Annual meeting location 1931: Boston, Massachusetts
Annual meeting location 1932: Louisville, Kentucky
Honorary member: Harvey Cushing
Membership: 31

John F. Fulton, PhD
1933–1934
Annual meeting location: St. Louis, Missouri

R. Glen Spurling, MD
1934–1935
Annual meeting location: New Haven, Connecticut

Merrill C. Sosman, MD
1935–1936
Annual meeting location: Rochester, Minnesota
Honorary members: Herbert Olivecrona, MD, and Ernest
        Sachs, MD

Kenneth G. McKenzie, MD
1936–1937
Annual meeting location: Philadelphia, Pennsylvania
Honorary member: Sir Geoffrey Jefferson, MD

Temple Fay, MD
1937–1938
Annual meeting location: Memphis, Tennessee

Louise Eisenhardt, MD
1938–1939
Annual meeting location: New Haven, Connecticut
Note: Held in honor of Cushing's 70th birthday

R. Eustace Semmes, MD
1939–1940
Annual meeting location: Kansas City, Missouri
Honorary member: Alfred W. Adson, MD

Cornelius G. Dyke, MD
1940–1941
Annual meeting location: Rochester, New York

Tracy J. Putnam, MD
1941–1942
Annual meeting location: New York, New York

Eric Oldberg, MD, PhD
1942–1943
Annual meeting location: New York, New York

Edgar F. Fincher Jr., MD
1943–1944
Annual meeting location: New York, New York
Honorary member: Howard C. Naffziger, MD

Franc D. Ingraham, MD
1944–1946
1945 Annual meeting location: Cancelled due to
    World War II
1946 Annual meeting location: Boston, Massachusetts

Frank R. Teachenor, MD
1946–1947
Annual meeting location: Hot Springs, Virginia

Cobb Pilcher, MD
1947–1948
Annual meeting location: San Francisco, California
Presidential address: "Neurosurgery Comes of Age."
        JNeurosurg 5:507-513, 1948
Honorary member: Eduard A. V. Busch, MD

Winchell McK. Craig, MD
1948–1949
Annual meeting location: New Haven, Connecticut

Frank T. Turnbull, MD
1949–1950
Annual meeting location: Colorado Springs, Colorado
Presidential address: "Neurosurgery is What You Make it."
        JNeurosurg 7:289–293, 1950

W. Edward Chamberlain, MD
1950–1951
Annual meeting location: Hollywood, Florida

Paul C. Bucy, MD
1951–1952
Annual meeting location: Victoria, British Columbia,
    Canada
Presidential Address: "Our Training Programs and
    the Future of Neurological Surgery." JNeurosurg
    9:538–543,1952

William J. German, MD
1952–1953
Annual meeting location: Hollywood, Florida
Presidential address: "The Place of Neurological Surgery
    in the Undergraduate Curriculum." JNeurosurg
    14:475–483, 1957.

Edgar A. Kahn, MD
1953–1954
Annual meeting location: Santa Fe, New Mexico
Membership: 407

Harry Wilkins, MD
1954–1955
Annual meeting location: Chateau Frontenac, Quebec,
    Canada
Honorary member: Norman M. Dott, MB, ChB, FRCS
Membership: 448

Frederick Schreiber, MD
1955–1956
Annual meeting location: Honolulu, Hawaii
Membership: 508

Leo M. Davidoff, MD
1956–1957
Annual meeting location: Detroit, Michigan
Membership: 516

Howard A. Brown, MD
1957–1958
Annual meeting location: Washington, D.C.
Presidential address: "The Harvey Cushing Society: Past,
    Present and Future." JNeurosurg 15:587–601, 1958.
Membership: 588

Bronson S. Ray, MD
1958–1959
Annual meeting location: New Orleans, Louisiana
Presidential address: "The Neurosurgeon's New Interest
    in the Pituitary." JNeurosurg 17:1–21, 1960
Membership: 668

James L. Poppen, MD
1959–1960
Annual meeting location: San Francisco, California
Presidential address: "Neurosurgery in the Soviet Union."
    JNeurosurg 17:573–582, 1960.
Membership: 708

J. Grafton Love, MD
1960–1961
Annual meeting location: Mexico City, Mexico
Presidential address: "Neurosurgery, The Public and the
    Law." JNeurosurg 18:567–576, 1961.
Membership: 760

Leonard T. Furlow, MD
1961–1962
Annual meeting location: Chicago, Illinois
Presidential address: "The American Board of Neurological
    Surgery." JNeurosurg 19:617–625, 1962.
Membership: 797

David L. Reeves, MD
1962–1963
Annual meeting location: Philadelphia, Pennsylvania
Presidential address: "The Harvey Cushing Library."
    JNeurosurg 20:545–556, 1963
Membership: 861

Barnes Woodhall, MD
1963–1964
Annual meeting location: Los Angeles, California
Presidential address: "Government, Medicine and the
    Common Wealth." JNeurosurg 21:827–834, 1964.
Membership: 917

Frank H. Mayfield, MD
1964–1965
Annual meeting location: New York, New York
Presidential address: "A Proclamation." JNeurosurg
    23:129–34, 1965.
Cushing Orator: Louise Eisenhardt, MD, managing
    editor, *Journal of Neurosurgery.* The First Annual
    Cushing Oration. JNeurosurg 22:224–228, 1965.
Award: Cushing Medal—Louise Eisenhardt, MD
Membership: 990

Francis Murphey, MD
1965–1966
Annual meeting location: St. Louis, Missouri
Presidential address: "Neurosurgery in American Medical
    Schools." JNeurosurg26:289–296, 1967.
Cushing Orator: Philip Handler, PhD, Duke University
    Medical Center. "Science and Public Policy."
    JNeurosurg 25:247–256, 1966.
Membership: 935

Eben Alexander Jr., MD
1966–1967
Annual meeting location: San Francisco, California
Presidential address: "Perspective on Neurosurgery."
    JNeurosurg 27:189–206, 1967.
Cushing orator: William H. Stewart, MD, Surgeon Gen-
    eral, Public Health Service, Department of Health,
    Education and Welfare. "The Responsibilities of
    Excellence." JNeurosurg 26:565–568, 1967.
Honorary Member: Oscar Hirsch, MD
Membership: 1,084

Henry G. Schwartz, MD
1967–1968
Annual meeting location: Chicago, Illinois
Presidential address: "Today's Needs and Neurosurgery's
    Response." JNeurosurg 29:221–228, 1968.
Cushing orator: R. Buckminster Fuller, PhD, architect and
    philosopher. [Not published]
Membership: 1,172

Donald D. Matson, MD
1968–1969
Annual meeting location: Cleveland, Ohio (Historical note: Dr. Matson died just before the annual meeting.)
Cushing orator: John S. Millis, PhD, vice president, National Fund for Medical Education. "The Paradox of Medical Practice and Medical Education." JNeurosurg 31:485–489, 1969.
Honorary members: Dorothy Russell, MD, and R. Eustace Semmes, MD (charter member)
Membership: 1,263

A. Earl Walker, MD
1969–1970
Annual meeting location: Washington, D.C.
Presidential address: "The Unresting Specialty." JNeurosurg 33:613-624, 1970.
Cushing orator: Edwin L. Crosby, MD, president, American Hospital Association. "The Changing Role of the Institution in Health Care." JNeurosurg 33:625–631, 1970.
Honorary Member: Wilder Penfield, MD
Membership: 1,335

Collin S. MacCarty, MD
1970–1971
Annual meeting location: Houston, Texas
Presidential address: "Past Personalities and Present Problems." JNeurosurg 35:633–645, 1971.
Cushing orator: Wilder Penfield, MD, Montreal Neurological Institute. "Lights in the Great Darkness." JNeurosurg 35:377–383, 1971.
Membership: 1,436

Guy L. Odom, MD
1971–1972
Annual meeting location: Boston, Massachusetts
Presidential address: "Neurological Surgery in Our
    Changing Times." JNeurosurg 37:255–268, 1972.
Cushing orator: Robert Q. Marston, MD, director,
    National Institutes of Health. "Biomedical Research
    Support Today." JNeurosurg 37:269–274, 1972.
Membership: 1,568

William F. Meacham, MD
1972–1973
Annual meeting location: Los Angeles, California
Presidential address: "The American Association of
    Neurological Surgeons and the Era of Issues."
    JNeurosurg 39:555–562, 1973.
Cushing orator: Wernher von Braun, PhD, vice president,
    engineering and development, Fairchild Industries.
    "The Future of the United States Space Program."
    JNeurosurg 39:135–144, 1973.
Membership: 1,595

Lyle A. French, MD
1973–1974
Annual meeting location: St. Louis, Missouri
Presidential address: "Some Issues in Health Education
    and Delivery of Health Care." JNeurosurg 41:
    409–414, 1974.
Cushing Orator: Malcolm Moos, PhD, president,
    University of Minnesota. [Not published]
Membership: 1,759

Richard C. Schneider, MD
1974–1975
Annual meeting location: Miami, Florida
Presidential address: "The 'Future Trends' in Neurosur-
    gery are Here." JNeurosurg 43:651–660, 1975.
Cushing orator: Paul W. McCracken, PhD, chairman,
    Department of Business Administration, University
    of Michigan. "Our Underpinnings: A Bicentennial
    View." JNeurosurg 43:515–522, 1975.
Honorary members: Gerard Guiot, MD, Hugo Krayen-
    buhl, MD, Gosta Norlen, MD, and Keiji Sano, MD
Membership: 1,905

Richard L. DeSaussure Jr., MD
1975–1976
Annual meeting location: San Francisco, California
Presidential address: "Assessment, Accomplishments,
    and Anxieties." JNeurosurg 45:601–608, 1976.
Cushing orator: Roger O. Egeberg, MD, special assistant
    to the secretary for health policy, Department of
    Health, Education and Welfare. "Medicine through
    Untinted Glasses." JNeurosurg 45:369–375, 1976.
Membership: 1,932

Lester A. Mount, MD
1976–1977
Annual meeting location: Toronto, Ontario, Canada
Presidential address: "Neurosurgery 1977: Problems and
    Attainments." JNeurosurg 47:647–652, 1977.
Cushing orator: Eli Ginzberg, PhD, director, conservation
    of human resources, Columbia University. "Man-
    power for Neurosurgery: Seeing Ourselves as Others
    See Us." JNeurosurg 47:803-809, 1977.
Award: Cushing Medal—Frank H. Mayfield, MD
Membership: 1,967

Charles G. Drake, MD
1977–1978
Annual meeting location: New Orleans, Louisiana
Presidential address: "Neurosurgery: Considerations for
    Strength and Quality." JNeurosurg 49:483–501, 1978.
Cushing Orator: C. Rollins Hanlon, MD, director,
    American College of Surgeons. "The Rhetoric of
    Specialization." JNeurosurg 49:785–793, 1978.
Award: Cushing Medal—William H. Sweet, MD
Membership: 2,153

Donald F. Dohn, MD
1978–1979
Annual meeting location: Los Angeles, California
Presidential address: "Neurosurgery at the Crossroads:
    Leadership Role of the American Association of Neu-
    rological Surgeons." JNeurosurg 51:429–436, 1979.
Cushing Orator: The Honorable Paul G. Rogers, attorney
    at law. [Not published]
Award:Cushing Medal—Henry G. Schwartz, MD
Membership: 2,260

W. Eugene Stern, MD
1979–1980
Annual meeting location: New York, New York
Presidential address: "A Nobleness of Purpose."
    JNeurosurg 53:137–143, 1980.
Cushing Orator: The Honorable Kingman Brewster,
    United States ambassador to Great Britain. "Is
    the Dream of a Voluntary Society Still Possible?"
    JNeurosurg 53:279–284, 1980.
Award: Cushing Medal—Paul C. Bucy, MD
Membership: 2,388

Robert B. King, MD
1980–1981
Annual meeting location: Boston, Massachusetts
Presidential address: "Traditions, Transition, and the
	Torch." JNeurosurg 55:329–336, 1981.
Cushing Orator: Julius Axelrod, PhD, chief, Section on
	Pharmacology, Laboratory of Clinical Science of
	NIH. "Catecholamine, Neurotransmitters, Psycho-
	active Drugs and Biological Clocks." JNeurosurg
	55:669, 1981.
Award: Cushing Medal—Bronson S. Ray, MD
Membership: 2,466

W. Kemp Clark, MD
1981–1982
Annual Meeting Location: Honolulu, Hawaii
Presidential address: "Structure and Function: Organiza-
	tion of a Medical Specialty for the Rest of the 20th
	Century." JNeurosurg 57:301–308, 1982.
Cushing Orator: Mortimor J. Adler, PhD, professor of
	philosophy and law, University of Chicago. "Minds
	and Brains: Angels, Humans and Brutes." JNeuro-
	surg 57:309, 1982
Award: Cushing Medal—W. James Gardner, MD
Membership: 2,585

Frank P. Wrenn, MD
1982–1983
Annual meeting location: Washington, D.C.
Presidential address: "Neurosurgery in the Eighties:
	A Challenge." Neurosurg 59:189–194, 1983.
Cushing Orator: Edmund D. Pelligrino, MD, professor
	of medicine and medical humanities, Georgetown
	University. "The Common Devotion—Cushing's
	Legacy and Medical Ethics." JNeurosurg 59:567,
	1983.
Award: Cushing Medal—Guy L. Odom, MD
Honorary member: Elizabeth C. Crosby, MD
Membership: 2,711

Byron C. Pevehouse, MD
1983–1984
Annual meeting location: San Francisco, California
Presidential address: "Residency Training in Neurological
    Surgery, 1934-1984: Evolution over 50 Years of Trial
    and Tribulation." JNeurosurg 61:999–1004, 1984.
Cushing Orator: Robert M. Rosenzweig, PhD, president,
    Association of American Universities. "Politics and
    Health: An Emerging Technology." JNeurosurg
    61:625, 1984.
Award: Cushing Medal—Eben Alexander Jr., MD
Honorary members: Lindsay Symon, MD, and Kurt-
    Friedrich Schurmann, MD
Membership: 2,798

Sidney Goldring, MD
1984–1985
Annual meeting location: Atlanta, Georgia
Presidential address: "The Need to Trace our Roots in
    Difficult Times." JNeurosurg 63:485–491, 1985.
Cushing Orator: Raymond E. Arvidson, PhD, professor of
    earth and planetary sciences, Washington University,
    St. Louis. "From Exploration of the Solar System to
    Utilization of Space Materials." JNeurosurg 63:317,
    1985.
Award: Cushing Medal—Francis Murphey, MD
Membership: 2,863

Russel H. Patterson Jr., MD
1985–1986
Annual meeting location: Denver, Colorado
Presidential address: "A Code of Ethics." JNeurosurg
    65:271–277, 1986.
Cushing Orator: The Honorable Richard D. Lamm, gover-
    nor of Colorado. "Infinite Needs: Finite Resources."
    JNeurosurg 65:435, 1986.
Award: Cushing Medal—Lyle French, MD
Honorary members: F. John Gillingham, MD, Murray
    Goldstein, MD, Hajime Handa, MD, and Shozo Ishii,
    MD
Membership: 2,916

Robert G. Ojemann, MD
1986–1987
Annual meeting location: Dallas, Texas
Presidential address: "The Tradition of Harvey Cushing
    Commemorated by a Stamp in the Great American
    Stamp Series." JNeurosurg 67:631–642, 1987.
Cushing Orator: H. Ross Perot, businessman. "Meeting
    International Competition." [Not published]
Awards: Cushing Medal—William F. Meacham, MD
    Humanitarian—Courtland H. Davis Jr., MD
Honorary members: Alexander N. Konovalov, MD, Wil-
    lem Luyendijk, MD, Emil Pasztor, MD, and Bernard
    Pertuiset, MD
Membership: 2,975

Henry D. Garretson, MD
1987–1988
Annual meeting location: Toronto, Ontario, Canada
Presidential address: "Utilization of Resources for the
    Maintenance of Excellence in Neurological Surgery."
    JNeurosurg 69:815–825, 1988.
Cushing Orator: The Honorable Brian Dickson, chief
    justice of the Supreme Court of Canada. "Law and
    Medicine: Conflict or Collaboration?" JNeurosurg
    69:319, 1988.
Awards: Cushing Medal—Charles G. Drake, MD
    Humanitarian—Gaston Acosta-Rua, MD
Honorary Members: Karl August Busche, MD, Brigadier
    Ramamurthi, MD, and Chung-Cheng Wang, MD
Membership: 3,082

George T. Tindall, MD
1988–1989
Annual meeting location: Washington, D.C.
Presidential address: "Trends in Neurosurgery."
    JNeurosurg 71:471480, 1989.
Cushing Orator: Theodore Cooper, MD, PhD, chair-
    man of the board and chief executive officer of the
    Upjohn Company. "Who is Managing the Manag-
    ers?" JNeurosurg 71:311, 1989.
Awards: Cushing Medal—Lester A. Mount, MD
    Humanitarian—Hugo V. Rizzoli, MD
Honorary Member: M. Gazi Yasargil, MD
Membership: 3,149

Albert L. Rhoton Jr., MD
1989–1990
Annual meeting location: Nashville, Tennessee
Presidential address: "Neurosurgery in the Decade of the
  Brain." JNeurosurg 73:487–495, 1990.
Cushing Orator: Jimmy Carter, former president of the
  United States. "Role of the United States in a Chang-
  ing World." JNeurosurg 73:813–819, 1990.
Awards: Cushing Medal—Robert B. King, MD
  Humanitarian—A. Roy Tyrer Jr., MD
Honorary Members: Andrei P. Romodanov, MD, and
  Henri Alphons D. Walder, MD
Lecture: Schneider—Robert G. Ojemann, MD
Membership: 3,267

David L. Kelly Jr., MD
1990–1991
Annual meeting location: New Orleans, Louisiana
Presidential address: "Now is Our Time." JNeurosurg
  75:677–685, 1991.
Cushing Orator: Yevgeny A. Yevtushenko, poet. "Everyone
  is Guilty in Everything." JNeurosurg 75:989–996, 1991.
Awards: Cushing Medal—William F. Collins, MD
  Humanitarian—George B. Udvarhelyi, MD
Lecture: Schneider—Jacques Moret, MD
Membership: 3,445

James T. Robertson, MD
1991–1992
Annual meeting location: San Francisco, California
Presidential address: "The AANS: The National and Inter-
  national Organization for Neurological Surgery."
  JNeurosurg 77:663–668, 1992.
Cushing Orator: Susan Eisenhower, director, Center for
  the Study of Soviet Change, and Roald Z. Sagdeev,
  PhD, distinguished professor of physics, University
  of Maryland. "The Post Cold War World." [Not
  published]
Awards: Cushing Medal—W. Eugene Stern, MD
  Humanitarian—William H. Mosberg Jr., MD
Honorary member: Madjid Samii, MD
Lecture: Schneider —Charles Wilson, MD
Membership: 3,729

Merwyn Bagan, MD
1992–1993
Annual meeting location: Boston, Massachusetts
Presidential address: "The Yin and Yang" of Neurological
    Surgery. JNeurosurg 79:807–809, 1993.
Cushing Orator: The Honorable Morris B. Abram, lawyer,
    educator, civil rights activist, diplomat. "The Ethics
    of Health Care Reform." [Not published]
Awards: Cushing Medal—Sidney Goldring, MD
    Distinguished Service—Roy W. Black, MD
    Humanitarian—Manuel Velasco-Suarez, MD
Lecture: Schneider—David L. Kelly Jr., MD
Membership: 3,904

Julian T. Hoff, MD
1993–1994
Annual meeting location: San Diego, California
Presidential address: "Toward Better Balance."
    JNeurosurg 81:651–655, 1994.
Cushing Orator: Beverly Sills, opera star and national
    chairwoman of the March of Dimes. "An Afternoon
    with Beverly Sills." [Not published]
Awards: Cushing Medal—Byron C. Pevehouse, MD
    Distinguished Service—William A. Buchheit, MD
    Humanitarian—E. Fletcher Eyster, MD
Lecture: Schneider—Jacque J. Sokolov, MD
Membership: 4,182

Edward L. Seljeskog, MD, PhD
1994–1995
Annual meeting location: Orlando, Florida
Presidential address: "Responding to the Challenge: The
    Challenge of the 1990s." JNeurosurg 83:771–777, 1995.
Cushing Orator: General Colin Powell, retired, chairman,
    Joint Chiefs of Staff. "The Management of Crisis and
    Change." [Not published]
Awards: Cushing Medal—Richard DeSaussure, MD
    Distinguished Service—Charles Edwin Bracket, MD
    Humanitarian—Melvin L. Cheatham, MD
Honorary Members: Roy W. Black, MD, and John W.
    Holter, MD
Lecture: Schneider—Michael L. J. Apuzzo, MD
Membership: 4,603

Sidney Tolchin, MD
1995–1996
Annual meeting location: Minneapolis, Minnesota
Presidential address: "The Worth of a Neurosurgeon." JNeurosurg 85:745–750, 1996.
Cushing Orator: William F. Buckley Jr., author, columnist, politician, advisor, adventurer, editor, philosopher, television personality, lecturer, political commentator. "Reflections on Current Contentious." [Not Published]
Awards: Cushing Medal—Shelley N. Chou, MD
    Distinguished Service—Robert E. Florin, MD, and Ralph and Ala Isham
Lecture: Patrick J. Kelly, MD
Membership: 4,841

J. Charles Rich Jr., MD
1996–1997
Annual meeting location: Denver, Colorado
Presidential address: "In Times of Change Learners Inherit the Earth." JNeurosurg 87:659–666, 1997.
Cushing Orator: William J. Bennett, PhD, former U.S. secretary of education, author, politician, professor. "In Defense of Western Civilization." [Not published]
Awards: Cushing Medal—Robert G. Ojemann, MD
    Distinguished Service—Ernest W. Mack, MD
    Humanitarian—Robert J. White, MD
Honorary Member: Carl H. Hauber, JD, CAE
Lecture: Schneider—L. N. Hopkins, MD
Membership: 5,086

Edward R. Laws Jr., MD
1997–1998
Annual meeting location: Philadelphia, Pennsylvania
Presidential address: "A Neurosurgical Way of Life." JNeurosurg 89:901–910, 1998
Cushing Orator: Eric Wieschaus, PhD, co-winner of the 1995 Nobel Prize. "What Fly Genes Can Tell Us about How Human Embroyos Develop." [Not published]
Awards: Cushing Medal—Albert L. Rhoton Jr., MD
    Distinguished Service—Mark J. Kubala, MD
    Humanitarian—Lee Finney, MD
Lecture: Schneider—Robert F. Spetzler, MD
Membership: 5,386

Russell L. Travis, MD
1998–1999
Annual meeting location: New Orleans, Louisiana
Presidential address: "Is the Age of Heroes Gone?"
 JNeurosurg 91:531–537, 1999.
Cushing Orator: George Herbert Walker Bush, former
 United States president. [Not published]
Awards: Cushing Medal—David L. Kelly Jr., MD
 Distinguished Service—W. Ben Blackett, MD, JD
 Humanitarian—Thomas B. Flynn, MD
Lecture: Schneider—Mahlon R. DeLong, MD
Membership: 5,329

Martin H. Weiss, MD
1999–2000
Annual meeting location: San Francisco, California
Presidential address: "Neurosurgery: A Historical Pro-
 logue to the Future." JNeurosurg 93:733–737, 2000.
Cushing Orator: Doris Kearns Goodwin, historian,
 Pulitzer Prize-winning author, and former Harvard
 professor. "Leadership in the New Millennium."
 [Not published]
Awards: Cushing Medal—Russel H. Patterson Jr., MD
 Distinguished Service—George Ablin, MD, and
 Robert H. Wilkins, MD
 Humanitarian—Merwyn Bagan, MD
Lecture: Schneider—W. French Anderson, MD
Membership: 5,867

Stewart B. Dunsker, MD
2000–2001
Annual meeting location: Toronto, Ontario, Canada
Presidential address: "Give Neurosurgery a Place to Stand."
 JNeurosurg 95:927–932–2001.
Cushing Orator: Tom Brokaw, anchor and managing editor
 of NBC Nightly News. [Not published]
Awards: Cushing Medal—Julian T. Hoff, MD
 Distinguished Service—Donald H. Stewart Jr., MD,
 and Frank P. Smith, MD
 Humanitarian—Gary D. Vander Ark, MD
Lecture: Schneider—Albert L. Rhoton Jr., MD
Membership: 6,179

Stan Pelofsky, MD
2001–2002
Annual meeting location: Chicago, Illinois
Presidential address: "The Voice of Art and the Art
    of Medicine." JNeurosurg 97:1261–1268, 2002.
Cushing Orator: Benazir Bhutto, former prime minister of
    Pakistan. "The Need for Leadership in a Dangerous
    World." [Not published]
Awards: Cushing Medal—Edward R. Laws Jr., MD
    Distinguished Service—John A. Jane Sr., MD
    Humanitarian—Edgar M. Housepian, MD
Lectures: Hunt-Wilson—Edward R. Laws Jr., MD
    Rhoton Family—Richard G. Fessler, MD
    Schneider—Patrick J. Kelly, MD
Membership: 6,339

Roberto C. Heros, MD
2002–2003
Annual meeting location: San Diego, California
Presidential address: "Neurosurgical Education: the 'Other'
    Competencies." JNeurosurg 99:623–629, 2003.
Cushing Orator: Henry A. Kissinger, PhD, national security
    advisor for six years, secretary of state to two presi-
    dents, Nobel laureate for his role in negotiating the
    withdrawal of American forces from Vietnam. [Not
    published]
Awards: Cushing Medal—Stewart B. Dunsker, MD
    Distinguished Service—Troy M. Tippett, MD
Lectures: Bittner—Andrew H. Kaye, MD
    Hunt-Wilson—Fred H. Gage, MD
    Kurze—M. Gazi Yasargi, MD
    Rhoton Family—Rear Admiral James A. Johnson, MD
    Schneider—Madjid Samii, MD, PhD
    Van Wagenen—Neal F. Kassell, MD
Membership: 6,612

A. John Popp, MD
2003–2004
Annual meeting location: Orlando, Florida
Presidential address: "Music, Musicians, and the Brain:
    An Exploration of Musical Genius." JNeurosurg
    101:895–903, 2004.
Cushing Orator: Ken Burns, director, producer, co-writer,
    chief cinematographer, music director, and execu-
    tive producer of the landmark television series "The
    Civil War," biographer. [Not published]
Awards: Cushing Medal—John A. Jane Sr., MD
    Distinguished Service —John A. Kusske, MD
    Humanitarian: Charles L. Branch Sr., MD
Honorary member: Jacques Brotchi, MD
Lectures: Bittner—James T. Rutka, MD, PhD, FRCS
    Hunt-Wilson—Pasko Rakic, MD
    Kurze—Robert F. Spetzler, MD
    Rhoton Family—Uwe Reinhardt, MD
    Schneider—Regis W. Haid Jr., MD
    Van Wagenen—Anders Bjorklund, MD
Membership: 6,718

Robert A. Ratcheson, MD
2004–2005
Annual meeting location: New Orleans, Louisiana
Presidential address: "Fast Forwarding: The Evolution
    of Neurosurgery." JNeurosurg 103:585–590, 2005.
Cushing Orator: Edmund Morris, Pulitzer Prize biogra-
    pher, historical biographer. [Not published]
Awards: Cushing Medal—Martin H. Weiss, MD
    Distinguished Service—John C. Van Gilder, MD
    Humanitarian—Tetsuo Tatsumi, MD
Honorary Member: Armando J. Basso, MD, PhD
Lectures: Bittner —Darrell Bigner, MD, PhD
    Hunt-Wilson—Henry J. Peter Ralston, MD
    Kurze—Martin H. Weiss, MD
    Rhoton Family—Robert G. Grossman, MD
    Schneider—Julian T. Hoff, MD
    Van Wagenen—Charles Warlow, MD, PhD
Membership: 6,906

Fremont P. Wirth Jr., MD
2005–2006
Annual meeting location: San Francisco, California
Presidential address: "Meeting the Challenges of Neuro-
    surgery." JNeurosurg 105: 807-810, 2006.
Cushing Orator: George F. Will, political commentator
    and columnist. "The Political Argument Today."
    [Not published]
Awards: Cushing Medal—David G. Kline, MD
    Distinguished Service—Lyal Leibrock, MD
    Humanitarian—Gene E. Bolles, MD
Lectures: Bittner—Mitchel S. Berger, MD
    Hunt-Wilson—Arnold R. Kriegstein, MD, PhD
    Kurze—Mark Bernstein, MD, FRCSC
    Rhoton Family—Volker K.H. Sonntag, MD
    Schneider—Arthur L. Day, MD
    Van Wagenen—Michael Merzenich, PhD
Membership: 7,053

Donald O. Quest, MD
2006–2007
Annual Meeting Location: Washington, DC
Presidential Address: Naval Aviation and Neurosurgery:
    Traditions, Commonalities, and Lessons Learned
Cushing Orator: Thomas L. Friedman, Pulitzer Prize win-
    ning New York Times columnist and author
Awards: Cushing Medal – Robert G. Grossman, MD
    Distinguished Service – Mary Louise Sanderson
    Humanitarian – Benjamin Warf, MD
Lectures: Bittner – Joseph M. Piepmeier, MD
    Eisenhardt – Sally Ride, PhD
    Hunt-Wilson – Eric Kandel, MD
    Kurze – Michael Gazzaniga, PhD
    Rhoton Family – Lisa Randall, PhD
    Schneider – L. Nelson Hopkins III, MD
    Van Wagenen – Johannes Schramm, MD

Officers

THE STRUCTURE OF THE ASSOCIATION's governing body has evolved through the years as membership and activities have grown. Initially, there were three elected officers—president, vice president, and secretary/treasurer. In 1957 elected officers were expanded to the current five positions—president, president-elect, vice president, secretary, and treasurer.

1932–1933
William P. Van Wagenen, MD, president
R. Glen Spurling, MD, vice president
Tracy J. Putnam, MD, secretary-treasurer

1933–1934
John F. Fulton, PhD, president
Leo M. Davidoff, MD, vice president
R. Eustace Semmes, MD, secretary-treasurer

1934–1935
R. Glen Spurling, MD, president
Louise Eisenhardt, MD, secretary-treasurer

1935–1936
Merrill C. Sosman, MD, president
Kenneth G. McKenzie, MD, vice president
Louise Eisenhardt, MD, secretary-treasurer

1936–1937
Kenneth G. McKenzie, MD, president
Richard Meagher, MD, vice president
Louise Eisenhardt, MD, secretary-treasurer

1937–1938
Temple Fay, MD, president
Frederick L. Reichert, MD, vice president
Louise Eisenhardt, MD, secretary-treasurer

1938–1939
Louise Eisenhardt, MD, president
Frank R. Teachenor, MD, vice president
William J. German, MD, secretary-treasurer

1939–1940
R. Eustace Semmes, MD, president
Winchell McK. Craig, MD, vice president
Louise Eisenhardt, MD, secretary-treasurer

1940–1941
Cornelius G. Dyke, MD, president
Edgar F. Fincher Jr., MD, vice president
Louise Eisenhardt, MD, secretary-treasurer

1941–1942
Tracy J. Putnam, MD, president
Edgar A. Kahn, MD, vice president
Louise Eisenhardt, MD, secretary-treasurer

1942–1943
Eric Oldberg, MD, PhD, president
Franc D. Ingraham, MD, vice president
Louise Eisenhardt, MD, secretary-treasurer

1943–1944
Edgar F. Fincher Jr., MD, president
William J. German, MD, vice president
Louise Eisenhardt, MD, secretary-treasurer

1944–1945; 1945–1946
Franc D. Ingraham, MD, president
Gilbert C. Anderson, MD, vice president
Louise Eisenhardt, MD, secretary-treasurer

1946–1947
Frank R. Teachenor, MD, president
Frank Turnbull, MD, vice president
Louise Eisenhardt, MD, secretary-treasurer

1947–1948
Cobb Pilcher, MD, president
Hale Haven, MD, vice president
Louise Eisenhardt, MD, secretary-treasurer

1948–1949
Winchell McK. Craig, MD, president
Howard A. Brown, MD, vice president
Louise Eisenhardt, MD, secretary-treasurer

1949–1950
Frank T. Turnbull, MD, president
Frank H. Mayfield, MD, vice president
Louise Eisenhardt, MD, secretary-treasurer

1950–1951
W. Edward Chamberlain, MD, president
Harry Wilkins, MD, vice president
Louise Eisenhardt, MD, secretary-treasurer

1951–1952
Paul C. Bucy, MD, president
Frederick Schreiber, MD, vice president
Louise Eisenhardt, MD, secretary-treasurer

1952–1953

William J. German, MD, president

Edgar A. Kahn, MD, president-elect

Eldridge Campbell, MD, vice president

David L. Reeves, MD, secretary-treasurer

1953–1954

Edgar A. Kahn, MD, president

Harry Wilkins, MD, president-elect

Franklin Jelsma, MD, vice president

David L. Reeves, MD, secretary-treasurer

1954–1955

Harry Wilkins, MD, president

Frederick Schreiber, MD, Past president

Richard U. Light, MD, vice president

David L. Reeves, MD, secretary-treasurer

1955–1956

Frederick Schreiber, MD, president

Leo M. Davidoff, MD, president-elect

James G. Lyerly Sr., MD, vice president

David L. Reeves, MD, secretary-treasurer

1956–1957

Leo M. Davidoff, MD, president

Howard A. Brown, MD, president-elect

W. Gayle Crutchfield, MD, vice president

David L. Reeves, MD, secretary

Hendrik J. Svien, MD, treasurer

1957–1958

Howard A. Brown, MD, president

Bronson S. Ray, MD, president-elect

Wallace B. Hamby, MD, vice president
David. L. Reeves, MD, secretary
Hendrik J. Svien, MD, treasurer

1958–1959
Bronson S. Ray, MD, president
James L. Poppen, MD, president-elect
James W. Watts, MD, vice president
David L. Reeves, MD, secretary
Hendrik. J. Svien, MD, treasurer

1959–1960
James L. Poppen, MD, president
J. Grafton Love, MD, president-elect
Francis Murphey, MD, vice president
Hendrik J. Svien, MD, secretary
Eben Alexander Jr., MD, treasurer

1960–1961
J. Grafton Love, MD, president
Leonard T. Furlow, MD, president-elect
John Raaf, MD, vice president
Hendrik J. Svien, MD, secretary
Eben Alexander Jr., MD, treasurer

1961–1962
Leonard T. Furlow, MD, president
David L. Reeves, MD, president-elect
Joseph P. Evans, MD, vice president
Hendrik J. Svien, MD, secretary
Eben Alexander Jr., MD, treasurer

1962–1963

David L. Reeves, MD, president
Barnes Woodhall, MD, president-elect
W. James Gardner, MD, vice president
Eben Alexander Jr., MD, secretary
Benjamin Whitcomb, MD, treasurer

1963–1964

Barnes Woodhall, MD, president
Frank Mayfield, MD, president-elect
Dean H. Echols, MD, vice president
Eben Alexander Jr., MD, secretary
Benjamin Whitcomb, MD, treasurer

1964–1965

Frank H. Mayfield, MD, president
Francis Murphey, MD, president-elect
Edwin Boldrey, MD, vice president
Eben Alexander Jr., MD, secretary
Benjamin Whitcomb, MD, treasurer

1965–1966

Francis Murphey, MD, president
Eben Alexander Jr., MD, president-elect
Collin S. MacCarty, MD, vice president
Benjamin Whitcomb, MD, secretary
William F. Meacham, MD, treasurer

1966–1967

Eben Alexander Jr., MD, president
Henry G. Schwartz, MD, president-elect
Charles G. Drake, MD, vice president
Benjamin Whitcomb, MD, secretary
William R. Meacham, MD, treasurer

1967–1968

Henry G. Schwartz, MD, president

Donald D. Matson, MD, president-elect

Richard L. DeSaussure Jr., MD, vice president

Benjamin Whitcomb, MD, secretary

William F. Meacham, MD, treasurer

1968–1969

Donald D. Matson, MD, president

A. Earl Walker, MD, president-elect

Oscar Sugar, MD, vice president

William F. Meacham, MD, secretary

Gordon van den Noort, MD, treasurer

1969–1970

A. Earl Walker, MD, president

Collin S. MacCarty, MD, president-elect

Henry Heyl, MD, vice president

William F. Meacham, MD, secretary

Gordon van den Noort, MD, treasurer

1970–1971

Collin S. MacCarty, MD, president

Guy L. Odom, MD, president-elect

Robert B. King, MD, vice president

William F. Meacham, MD, secretary

Gordon van den Noort, MD, treasurer

1971–1972

Guy L. Odom, MD, president

William F. Meacham, MD, president-elect

Benjamin B. Whitcomb, MD, vice president

Gordon van den Noort, MD, secretary

Donald F. Dohn, MD, treasurer

1972–1973

William F. Meacham, MD, president

Lyle A. French, MD, president-elect

Richard Schneider, MD, vice president

Gordon van den Noort, MD, secretary

Donald F. Dohn, MD, treasurer

1973–1974

Lyle A. French, MD, president

Richard C. Schneider, MD, president-elect

George Roulhac, MD, vice president

Gordon van den Noort, MD, secretary

Donald F. Dohn, MD, treasurer

1974–1975

Richard C. Schneider, MD, president

Richard L. DeSaussure Jr., MD, president-elect

C. Douglas Hawkes, MD, vice president

Donald F. Dohn, MD, secretary

Charles E. Brackett, MD, treasurer

1975–1976

Richard L. DeSaussure Jr., MD, president

Lester A. Mount, MD, president-elect

Ernest W. Mack, MD, vice president

Donald F. Dohn, MD, secretary

Charles E. Brackett, MD, treasurer

1976–1977
Lester A. Mount, MD, president
Charles G. Drake, MD, president-elect
Russel H. Patterson Jr., MD, vice president
Donald F. Dohn, MD, secretary
Charles E. Brackett, MD, treasurer

1977–1978
Charles G. Drake, MD, president
Donald F. Dohn, MD, president-elect
John F. Mullan, MD, vice president
Charles E. Brackett, MD, secretary
Byron C. Pevehouse, MD, treasurer

1978–1979
Donald F. Dohn, MD, president
W. Eugene Stern, MD, vice president
Ross H. Miller, MD, vice president
Charles E. Brackett, MD, secretary
Byron C. Pevehouse, MD, treasurer

1979–1980
W. Eugene Stern, MD, president
Robert B. King, MD, president-elect
Robert L. McLaurin, MD, vice president
Charles E. Brackett, MD, secretary
Byron C. Pevehouse, MD, treasurer

1980–1981
Robert B. King, MD, president
W. Kemp Clark, MD, president-elect
Richard L. Rovit, MD, vice president
Byron C. Pevehouse, MD, secretary
Bruce F. Sorensen, MD, treasurer

1981–1982

W. Kemp Clark, MD, president

Frank R. Wren, MD, president-elect

George Ablin, MD, vice president

Byron C. Pevehouse, MD, secretary

Bruce F. Sorenson, MD, treasurer

1982–1983

Frank R. Wrenn, MD, president

Byron C. Pevehouse, MD, president-elect

Hugo V. Rizzoli, MD, vice president

Edward L. Seljeskog, MD, PhD, secretary

Bruce F. Sorenson, MD, treasurer

1983–1984

Byron C. Pevehouse, MD, president

Sidney Goldring, MD, president-elect

William E. Hunt, MD, vice president

Edward L. Seljeskog, MD, PhD, secretary

Albert L. Rhoton Jr., MD, treasurer

1984–1985

Sidney Goldring, MD, president

Russel H. Patterson Jr., MD, president-elect

Shelly N. Chou, MD, vice president

Edward L. Seljeskog, MD, PhD, secretary

Albert L. Rhoton Jr., MD, treasurer

1985–1986

Russel H. Patterson Jr., MD, president

Robert G. Ojemann, MD, president-elect

Thomas W. Langfitt, MD, vice president

Henry D. Garretson, MD, secretary

Albert L. Rhoton Jr., MD, treasurer

1986–1987

Robert G. Ojemann, MD, president

Henry D. Garretson, MD, president-elect

George T. Tindall, MD, vice president

David L. Kelly Jr., MD, secretary

James T. Robertson, MD, treasurer

1987–1988

Henry D. Garretson, MD, president

George T. Tindall, MD, president-elect

Albert L. Rhoton Jr., MD, vice president

David L. Kelly Jr., MD, secretary

James T. Robertson, MD, treasurer

1988–1989

George T. Tindall, MD, president

Albert L. Rhoton Jr., MD, president-elect

David L. Kelly Jr., MD, vice president

Sidney Tolchin, MD, secretary

James T. Robertson, MD, treasurer

1989–1990

Albert L. Rhoton Jr., MD, president

David L. Kelly Jr., MD, president-elect

James T. Robertson, MD, vice president

Sidney Tolchin, MD, secretary

Robert H. Wilkins, MD, treasurer

1990–1991

David L. Kelly Jr., MD, president

James T. Robertson, MD, president-elect

Donald H. Stewart Jr., MD, vice president

Sidney Tolchin, MD, secretary

Robert H. Wilkins, MD, treasurer

1991–1992

James T. Robertson, MD, president

Merwyn Bagan, MD, president-elect

Julian T. Hoff, MD, vice president

J. Charles Rich Jr., MD, secretary

Robert H. Wilkins, MD, treasurer

1992–1993

Merwyn Bagan, MD, president

Julian T. Hoff, MD, president-elect

Sidney Tolchin, MD, vice president

J. Charles Rich Jr., MD, secretary

Edward R. Laws Jr., MD, treasurer

1993–1994

Julian T. Hoff, MD, president

Edward L. Seljeskog, MD, PhD, president-elect

Charles B. Wilson, MD, vice president

J. Charles Rich Jr., MD, secretary

Edward R. Laws Jr., MD, treasurer

1994–1995

Edward L. Seljeskog, MD, PhD, president

Sidney Tolchin, MD, president-elect

Donald O. Quest, MD, vice president

Martin H. Weiss, MD, secretary

Edward R. Laws Jr., MD, treasurer

1995–1996

Sidney Tolchin, MD, president

J. Charles Rich Jr., MD, president-elect

William A. Buchheit, MD, vice president

Martin H. Weiss, MD, secretary

Stewart B. Dunsker, MD, treasurer

1996–1997

J. Charles Rich Jr., MD, president

Edward R. Laws Jr., MD, president-elect

Russell L. Travis, MD, vice president

Martin H. Weiss, MD, secretary

Stewart B. Dunsker, MD, treasurer

1997–1998

Edward R. Laws Jr., MD, president

Russell L. Travis, MD, president-elect

William S. Shucart, MD, vice president

Stewart B. Dunsker, MD, treasurer

Stan Pelofsky, MD, secretary

1998–1999

Russell L. Travis, MD, president

Martin H. Weiss, MD, president-elect

Stewart B. Dunsker, MD, vice president

Roberto C. Heros, MD, treasurer

Stan Pelofsky, MD, secretary

1999–2000

Martin H. Weiss, MD, president

Stewart B. Dunsker, MD, president-elect

A. John Popp, MD, vice president

Stan Pelofsky, MD, secretary

Roberto C. Heros, MD, treasurer

2000–2001

Stewart B. Dunsker, MD, president

Stan Pelofsky, MD, president-elect

John A. Kusske, MD, vice president

Robert A. Ratcheson, MD, secretary

Roberto C. Heros, MD, treasurer

2001–2002

Stan Pelofsky, MD, president

Roberto C. Heros, MD, president-elect

Volker Sonntag, MD, vice president

Robert A. Ratcheson, MD, secretary

Arthur L. Day, MD, treasurer

2002–2003

Roberto C. Heros, MD, president

A. John Popp, MD, president-elect

Fremont P. Wirth Jr., MD, vice president

Robert A. Ratcheson, MD, secretary

Arthur L. Day, MD, treasurer

2003–2004

A. John Popp, MD, president

Robert A. Ratcheson, MD, president-elect

Randall W. Smith, MD, vice president

Jon H. Robertson, MD, secretary

Arthur L. Day, MD, treasurer

2004–2005

Robert A. Ratcheson, MD, president

Fremont P. Wirth Jr., MD, president-elect

Charles J. Hodge Jr., MD, vice president

Jon H. Robertson, MD, secretary

James R. Bean, MD, treasurer

2005–2006

Fremont P. Wirth Jr., MD, president

Donald O. Quest, MD, president-elect

Robert L. Grubb Jr., MD, vice president

Jon H. Robertson, MD, secretary

James R. Bean, MD, treasurer

2006–2007

Donald O. Quest, MD, president

Jon H. Robertson, MD, president-elect

Arthur L. Day, MD, vice president

James T. Rutka, MD PhD, secretary

James R. Bean, MD, treasurer

Journal of Neurosurgery Editors and Editorial Board Chairmen

SINCE ITS INITIAL ISSUE IN 1944, THE *Journal of Neurosurgery* has continually benefited from the guidance and support of the Editorial Board, whose members and dates of service are listed below.

Editors

Louise Eisenhardt, MD (1944–1965)

Henry Heyl, MD (1965–1975)

Henry Schwartz, MD (1975–1985)

William Collins Jr., MD (1985–1990)

Thoralf Sundt Jr., MD (1990–1992)

John A. Jane Sr., MD, PhD (1992–)

Chairmen

Gilbert Horrax, MD, Boston, Massachusetts (1944–1950)

R. Glen Spurling, MD, Louisville, Kentucky (1951–1952)

Kenneth G. McKenzie, MD, Toronto, Ontario (1953–1954)

Winchell McK. Craig, MD, Rochester, Minnesota (1955–1956)

Paul C. Bucy, MD, Chicago, Illinois (1957–1960)

Barnes Woodhall, MD, Durham, North Carolina (1961–1962)

Bronson S. Ray, MD, New York, New York (1963–1964)

David L. Reeves, MD, Santa Barbara, California (l965–1966)

Henry G. Schwartz, MD, St. Louis, Missouri (1967–1968)

Eben Alexander Jr., MD, Winston-Salem, North Carolina (1969–1970)

Arthur A. Ward Jr., MD, Seattle, Washington (1971–1972)

Lyle A. French, MD, Minneapolis, Minnesota (1973–1974)

Charles G. Drake, MD, London, Ontario (1975–1976)

Sidney Goldring, MD, St. Louis, Missouri (1977–1978)

Thomas W. Langfitt, MD, Philadelphia, Pennsylvania (1979–1980)

Charles B. Wilson, MD, San Francisco, California (1981–1982)

John F. Mullan, MD, Chicago, Illinois (1983–1984)

W. Eugene Stern, MD, Los Angeles, California (1985–1986)

Thoralf M. Sundt Jr., MD, Rochester, Minnesota (1987–1988)

Robert G. Grossman, MD, Houston, Texas (1988–1989)

Nicholas T. Zervas, MD, Boston, Massachusetts (1989–1990)

John A. Jane Sr., MD, PhD, Charlottesville, Virginia (1990–1991)

George A. Ojemann, MD, Seattle, Washington (1991–1992)

Michael Pollay, MD, Oklahoma City, Oklahoma (1992–1993)

Bryce K. A. Weir, MD, Chicago, Illinois (1993–1994)

Robert L. Grubb Jr., MD, St. Louis, Missouri (1994–1995)

Martin H. Weiss, MD, Los Angeles, California (1995–1996)

Robert H. Wilkins, MD, Durham, North Carolina (1996–1997)

Co-chairmen began in 1997
Howard M. Eisenberg, MD, Baltimore, Maryland (1997–1999)

Julian T. Hoff, MD, Ann Arbor, Michigan (1997–1999)

John P. Girvin, MD, London Ontario Canada (1999–2000)

Donald P. Becker, MD, Los Angeles, California (1999–2000)

Robert A. Ratcheson, MD, Cleveland, Ohio (2000–2001)

Charles J. Hodge Jr., MD, Syracuse, New York (2000–2001)

Edward H. Oldfield, MD, Bethesda, Maryland (2001–2002)

H. Richard Winn, MD, Seattle, Washington (2001–2002)

Ralph G. Dacey Jr., MD, St. Louis, Missouri (2002–2003)
Lawrence F. Marshall, MD, San Diego, California (2002–2003)

Edward C. Benzel, MD, Cleveland, Ohio (2003–2004)
James T. Rutka, MD, PhD, Toronto Ontario Canada (2003–2004)

Single chairmen, *Journal of Neurosurgery*:
David W. Roberts, MD, Lebanon, New Hampshire (2005)
Nicolas de Tribolet, MD, Genève, Switzerland (2006)

***Journal of Neurosurgery*: Pediatrics Chairmen:**
R. Michael Scott, MD, Boston, Massachusetts (2005)
Marion Walker, MD, Salt Lake City, Utah (2006)

***Journal of Neurosurgery*: Spine Chairmen:**
Volker K. H. Sonntag, MD, Phoenix, Arizona (2005)
Edward C. Benzel, MD, Cleveland, Ohio (2006)

Research Foundation/Neurosurgical Research and Education Foundation (NREF)

SINCE 1981, THE NEUROSURGERY RESEARCH and Education Foundation (founded as the Research Foundation) has been the premier funder of neurosurgical studies focusing on providing fellowship funding in basic neuroscience and neurosurgical programs in North America.

Executive Council Chairmen
Robert B. King, MD (1980–1991)
Robert G. Ojemann, MD (1991–1999)
Julian T. Hoff, MD (1999–2004)
Martin H. Weiss, MD (2004–2007)
Griffith R. Harsh, IV, MD (2007–)

Scientific Advisory Committee Chairman
Robert Grossman, MD (1983–)

Research Fellows (resident awards)
1983
Samuel J. Hassenbusch, MD, PhD, Johns Hopkins University
    Brain Tumor and Surrounding Brain Penetration by Non-
    Lipophilic Chemotherapeutic Agents in Brain Tumor Therapy
Robert M. Levy, MD, PhD, University of California/San Francisco
    The Effect of Opiates and Opiate Antagonists on Acute Cerebral
    Ischemia and Infarction

1984
Steven J. Schiff, MD, PhD, Duke University
    Study of the Protection of Neural Tissue During Hypoxia

1985
Joseph M. Phillips, MD, Massachusetts General Hospital
    Investigation of Two Sodium-Potassium-Stimulated ATPase's
    (Na-K ATPase) in Rat and Human Brain

1986
Griffith R. Harsh IV, MD, University of California/San Francisco
    The Role of Growth Factor Related Oncogenes in Central Nervous
    System Tumors

1988
John Aryanpur[1], MD, Johns Hopkins University
    Excitatory Amino Acid Mechanisms in the Mediation of Epilepsy
    and Anoxic-Ischemic Brain Injury

1989

Joung H. Lee, MD[1], University of Virginia
 Protective Effects of Hypothermia Following CNS Ischemia

Richard G. Parker, MD[5] (Deceased), University of Minnesota
 NGF and Grafted Adrenal Medulla in MPTP-Hemiparkinsonism

1990

Michael M. Haglund, MD, PhD, University of Washington
 Video Imaging of Neuronal Activity with Voltage-Sensitive
 Dyes in Chronic Monkey Epileptic Foci

1991

Gregory A. Brandenberg, MD, PhD, University of Missouri
 An Investigation into the Effects of Peripheral Nerve Injury on the
 Response Properties of Neurons in the Somatosensory Cortex

E. Thomas Chappell, MD, George Washington University
 Glial Tumor Cell Motility: The Role of Surface Enzymes

1992

Mark S. LeDoux, MD, University of Alabama
 Cerebellar Output and its Control in a Dystonia Model

Stephen L. Skirboll, MD, University of Washington
 Transgenic Grafts in Experimental Parkinsonism

1993

John Paul Elliott, MD, University of Washington
 Function of Type I Sodium Channel

1994

James D. Guest, MD, PhD[2], University of Miami
 Significance and Treatment of Demyelination in Human
 Spinal Cord Injury

William D. Hunter, MD, Georgetown University
    Genetically Engineered Herpes Simplex Virus Containing IL-4,
    IL-6, and Antisense IGF-1 and its Effects on Glioblastoma Cells

1995

D. Kyle Kim, MD, PhD[3], University of Washington
    Protein-Protein Interactions and N-Type Calcium Channel
    Function

John H. Sampson, MD, PhD, Duke University
    Evaluation of the Efficacy and Toxicity of Tumor-Specific Mono-
    clonal Antibodies that Recognize a Variant of the Epidermal
    Growth Factor Receptor on Human Malignant Gliomas

Frank Feigenbaum, MD, Georgetown University
    Transcriptional Targeting of Recombinant HSV for Treatment
    of Nestin Producing Brain Tumors

1996

Guy M. McKhann II, MD, PhD, University of Washington
    Regulation of Potassium and Extracellular Space by the Astrocytic
    Syncytium in Gliotic Hippocampus

1997

Lilyana Angelov, MD, University of Toronto
    Ras Activity and Expression of Vascular Endothelial Growth
    Factor in NF-1 Peripheral Nerve Tumors

Amy B. Heimberger, MD, Duke University
    Cytotoxic Lymphocyte Response against Central Nervous System
    Tumors

1998

Tord D. Alden, MD, University of Virginia
    Bone Morphogenetic Protein-2 Gene Therapy in Neurosurgery

Judith L. Gorelick, MD, University of Michigan
Role of the MXI1 Growth Suppressor Gene in the Pathogenesis
of Glioblastoma Multiforme

James M. Schuster, MD, PhD, University of Washington
Effects of Loss of p53 Function on Apoptotic Pathways in the
Malignant Progression of Astrocytes

1999

Gregory D. Foltz, MD[6], University of Washington
High Density cDNA Array Analysis of Gene Expression
in Astrocytic Tumors

Babak S. Jahromi, MD, PhD[7], University of Toronto
Electrophysiological Properties and Intracellular Ca2+
Homeostasis in Vasospastic Smooth Muscle

Sunghoon Lee, MD, Yale University
Long Term Modifications in the Human Hippocampus:
Implications for Human Memory

2000

Dean Chou, MD, Johns Hopkins Hospital
Inhibition of Angiogenesis by Knockout of Id1 and Id3 and
its Effects on Murine Brain Tumor Growth

John K. Park, MD, PhD, Brigham & Women's Hospitals
Prevention of Venous Thromboembolism in Brain Tumor Patients

Matthew D. Smyth, MD, University of California/San Francisco
Pharmacoresistance in an Animal Model of Cortical Dysplasia

Michael M. Woodruff, MD, University of Utah Medical Center
Neural Restoration after Radiation Injury

2001

Laurie L. Ackerman, MD[10], University of Iowa
GABAergic Mechanisms of Neuropathic Pain

Kent C. New, MD, PhD, Duke University Medical Center
Telomerase Vaccination for Therapy of Brain Tumors

Adetokunbo A. Oyelese, MD, PhD, Stanford University
Neural Transdifferentiation of Bone Marrow Stromal Cells

Michael Taylor, MD, PhD, University of Toronto
Role of Gli Transcription Factors in the Pathogenesis
of Medulloblastoma

2002

Robert Dodd, MD[11], Stanford University
The Role of KCA Channels in Chronic Cerebral Vasospasm

Sheila K. Singh, MD[8], University of Toronto
A Novel Assay of Stem Cells in Pediatric Brain Tumors

Ira Garonzik, MD[10], Johns Hopkins University
Laser Evoked Potentials to Study Human Cortical Pain-Signaling
Pathways in Patients with Implanted Grids and Central Nervous
System Lesions

Charles C. Matouk, MD, University of Toronto
Endothelial Phenotype in Inherited Neurovascular Disease:
Transgenic Approaches

2003

Ramin Amirnovin, MD, Massachusetts General Hospital
Interaction of the Subthalamic Nucleus and the Globus Pallidus
Interna in Movement Control

Robert J. Kowalski, MD[12], Cleveland Clinic
   An In Vitro Biomechanical Assessment of Motion Preservation
   Strategies for the Lumbar Spine

John S. Kuo, MD, PhD[8], University of Toronto
   Developing New Diagnostic and Therapeutic Strategies for
   Medulloblastoma Based on a Novel Tumor Specific Gene, OPL

Todd G. Mainprize, MD, University of Toronto
   The Role of GLI2 in the Pathogenesis of Medulloblastoma

Atom Sarkar, MD, PhD, Mayo Clinic
   Exploration of Bio-Mechanical Forces within the Central Nervous
   System

2004

David Cory Adamson, MD, PhD, Duke University
   Identification of Novel Molecular Therapeutic Markers in
   Glioblastoma Multiforme

Ryan DenHaese, MD, University of Maryland
   Molecular Mechanism for Adenosine Effects in Cerebral Vessels

Michael Kelly, MD[12], University of Saskatchewan
   Synchrotron-supported Imaging of Spinal Cord Injury in an
   Animal Model

Kendall Lee, MD[10], Dartmouth-Hitchcock
   Mechanism of Action of Deep Brain Stimulation

Brian Ragel, MD, University of Utah
   Cyclooxygenase-2 (COX-2) Inhibitors in the Treatment
   of Meningiomas

Michael Louis Smith, MD, University of Pennsylvania
Injury-induced Alterations of Hippocampal Function: Electrophysiologic Investigations of Circuit and Synaptic Signaling.

2005

Daniel P. Cahill, MD, PhD, Massachusetts General Hospital
Analysis of Oligodendroglioma Gene Expression Profiles

Ali Chahlavi, MD, Cleveland Clinic Foundation
GBM Immunotherapy with Desferoxamine

Suresh N. Magge, MD, University of Pennsylvania
The Role of Chemokines in Regulating Neuronal Stem Cell Migration towards Brain Tumors

Joseph G. Ong, MD[12], University of Pittsburgh
Design of a Human Cortical Neural Prosthetic

2006

Ming (David) Cheng, MD, University of North Carolina
The Role of the Primate Neostriatum in Learning Novel Visual-Motor Associations

Lewis Chun Hou, MD, Stanford University
Integrin avß3 based Molecular Imaging of Tumor Angiogenesis in a Mouse Post-Resection Glioblastoma Multiforme Model

Eric M. Jackson, MD, University of Pennsylvania
Chromosome 22 Deletions and Aberrant INI1 Expression in Pediatric and Adult Gliomas

Adrian W. Laxton, MD[10], University of Toronto
The Modulation of Cognitive Function Using Electrical Stimulation

Daniel A. Lim, MD, PhD, University of California/San Francisco
Role of the MII Chromatin Remodeling Gene in the Control
of Adult Brain Neural Stem Cells

Neil R. Malhotra, MD[12], University of Pennsylvania
Injectable Hydrogels to Support Nucleus Pulposus Function and
their Potential to Deliver Therapeutic Agents

Wael Musleh, MD, PhD, University of Chicago
The Role of Calpain-mediated Modification of Delayed-rectifier
Potassium Channels (Kv2.1) in Subarachnoid Hemorrhage-
induced Vasospasm

Lyman W. Whitlatch, MD[13], Duke University
Elastin-Laminin Copolymers for Intervertebral Disc Repair

1 Co-funded with the Head Trauma Foundation
2 Co-funded with the Joint Section on Disorders of the Spine and Peripheral Nerves
3 Co-funded with the Upjohn Company
4 Co-funded with the Joint Section of Pediatric Neurological Surgery
5 Deceased
6 Co-funded with Rhone Poulenc Rorer
7 Co-funded with a gift from the Shirley L. Bagan Trust
8 Co-funded with the American Brain Tumor Association
9 Co-funded with a gift from the Hunt-Wilson Trust
10 Co-funded with Medtronic Neurological
11 Co-funded with a gift from the Frank Z. Bagan Trust
12 Co-funded with DePuy Spine
13 Co-funded with Kyphon Inc.

Young Clinician Investigators (attending awards)

1986

Marc R. Mayberg, MD, University of Washington
    Piglet Model for Vasospasm after Subarachnoid Hemorrhage

Warren R. Selman, MD, Case Western Reserve
    Metabolic Alterations of Focal Cerebral Ischemia

1987

Roberta P. Glick, MD, University of Illinois
    Insulin and Insulin-like Growth Factor in Brain Tumors: Binding
    and In Vitro Effects

J. Marc Simard, MD, PhD, University of Texas
    Effects of CO_2 and pH on Calcium Currents in Cerebrovascular
    Cells

1988

Gary K. Steinberg, MD, PhD1, Stanford University
    Dextromethorphan and Dextrorphan in the Treatment of Focal
    Cerebral Ischemia

Julian K. Wu, MD, Tufts New England Medical Center
    Oncogenes in Astrocytomas

1989

Samuel J. Hassenbusch, MD, PhD, Cleveland Clinic
    Study of Novel Brain Tumor Drugs and Drug Diluents in a Rabbit
    Tumor Model

Fredric B. Meyer, MD, Mayo Clinic
    Evaluation of Relationship Between Neuronal Hyperexcitability
    and Ischemic Brain Injury

1990

M. Christopher Wallace, MD, University of Toronto
Effect of Focal Cerebral Ischemia on Secondary Messenger
Systems

1991

Kenneth Follett, MD, PhD, University of Iowa
Involvement of Cerebral Cortical Neurons in Visceral
Nociception

Jeffrey J. Olson, MD, Emory Clinic
Investigation of Basic Fibroblastic Growth Factor Release from
Extracellular Matrix by Malignant Brain Tumors

Eric L. Zager, MD, University of Pennsylvania
Cerebral Protection Against Focal Ischemia

1992

Ian Pollack, MD, University of Pittsburgh
The Role of Growth Factor Pathways in the Proliferation
of Pediatric Brain Tumors

1993

William T. Couldwell, MD, PhD, University of Southern California
Signal Transduction in Malignant Gliomas

Diana L. Abson Kraemer, MD, Yale University
Effects of Calcium Flux Within Astrocytes

1994

R. Loch Macdonald, MD, PhD, University of Chicago
Role of Free Radicals in Pathogenesis of Vasospasm Following
Subarachnoic Hemorrhage

Donald M. O'Rourke, MD, University of Pennsylvania
Signal Transduction in Malignant Gliomas

Abbas F. Sadikot, MD, Montreal Neurological Institute
Pattern Formation in the Mammalian Striatum: A Participation
of Thalamic Afferents

1995

Lawrence S. Chin, MD, University of Maryland
Potassium Channel Activity in Malignant Astrocytoma

Mark S. Dias, MD[4], State University of New York/Buffalo
Neuronal Proliferation and Programmed Cell Death of Spinal
Motoneurons in a Chick Embryo Model of Dysraphism

1996

James M. Markert Jr., MD, University of Alabama
Mutant Herpes Simplex Virus for IL-12 Cytokine Gene Therapy
of Glioma

1997

E. Sander Connolly Jr., MD, Columbia University
Leukocyte Adhesion Receptors and Thrombosis in the
Pathogenesis of Evolving Stroke

Adam Mamelak, MD, California Institute of Technology
Injury Induced Neuronal Reorganization in the Hippocampus

1998

Frederick F. Lang Jr., MD, Anderson Cancer Center
Adenovirus-mediated p53 Gene Transfer Combined with Ion-
izing Radiation and Antineoplastic Agents Against p53-Wild-Type
Human Gliomas

Carl Lauryssen, MD, Washington University
Computer Analysis Outcome Study of Cervical Spondylotic Myelopathy

1999

Robert E. Gross, MD, PhD, University of Utah
Role of the Netrins in the Generation and Regeneration of the Nigrostriatal Pathway

John H. Sampson, MD, PhD, Duke University
Determination of the Radiopharmacokinetics and Dose for Bulk Flow Microinfusion of 131-I-Labeled Antitenascin Monoclonal Antibody

2000

John K. Park, MD, PhD, Brigham & Women's Hospitals
Prevention of Venous Thromboembolism in Brain Tumor Patients

Bruce E. Pollock, MD[9], Mayo Clinic
Patient Outcomes after Vestibular Schwannoma Management: A Prospective Comparison of Surgical Resection and Stereotactic Radiosurgery

Michael A. Vogelbaum, MD, PhD, Cleveland Clinic Foundation
Mechanisms by which P53 Regulates Bax-induced Apoptosis in Human Gliomas

2001

Zelma H. T. Kiss, MD, PhD, University of Calgary
Cellular Mechanisms Underlying Deep Brain Stimulation (DBS) Therapy

Theodore H. Schwartz, MD, Cornell University
In Vivo Optical Mapping of the Dynamic Topography of the Epileptogenic Aggregate in Chronic Rodent Neocortical Epilepsy

2002

Jeffrey P. Blount, MD, University of Alabama
Magnetic Source Imaging and Magnetic Resonance Spectroscopy
in the Assessment of Medically Refractile Pediatric Epilepsy
Arising from Malformations of Cortical Development

Nicholas Boulis, MD, Cleveland Clinic Foundation
Phage Display and In Vivo Biopanning for Small Neurotropic
Peptides

2003

Judy Huang, MD, Johns Hopkins University
The Effects of Estrogen on Matrix Metalloproteinase-mediated
Inflammatory Injury in Stroke

Andrew T. Parsa, MD, PhD, University of California/San Francisco
Mechanisms Underlying Glioma Immunity

Kevin A. Walter, MD, University of Pittsburgh
Gene Expression in Brain Tumor Angiogenesis

2004

Maxwell Boakye, MD3, Stanford University
Differential Plasticity of Sensory and Motor Cortical Systems
in Patients with Spinal Cord Injury

Steven Casha, MD, PhD2, Foothills Hospital
Metalloproteinase Inhibition in Acute Spinal Cord Injury:
A Human Pilot Study of Intravenous Minocycline

Amy B. Heimberger, MD, University of Texas
Phenotypic and Functional Characterization of Microglia within
Malignant Gliomas

Charles Y. Liu, MD, PhD, University of Southern California
Artificial Niches for Neural Stem Cells

2005

Gavin W. Britz, MD, University of Washington
Cerebral Arteriolar Reactivity following Subarachnoid
Hemorrhage in a Mouse Model

William T. Curry Jr., MD, Massachusetts General Hospital
Herpes Simplex Virus Oncolytic Immunotherapy for Brain
Tumors

Emad Eskandar, MD, Massachusetts General Hospital
Role of Basal Ganglia in Visual-Motor Learning

James W. Leiphart, MD, PhD, George Washington University
Dorsal Root Ganglion and Spinal Cord Alpha2-Adrenergic
Receptors in Neuropathic Pain: A Binding Study

Stephen Russell, MD, New York University
Netrin-1 and the Homing Behavior of Regenerating Axons
in the Axolotl

2006

John Boockvar, MD[6], Weill Cornell Medical College
Mechanisms Underlying EGFR Mediated Human Adult
Progenitor Cell Invasion

Alfredo Quinones-Hinojosa, MD[5], Johns Hopkins University
Isolation, Characterization, Migration, and Transformation
of Human Subventricular Zone Neural Stem Cells

Michael D. Taylor, MD, PhD, Hospital for Sick Children
High Resolution Genotyping of Pediatric Medulloblastoma

G. Edward Vates, MD PhD, University of Rochester
Dysregulation of Functional Hyperemia after Subarachnoid
Hemorrhage

William P. Van Wagenen Fellowship

The William P. Van Wagenen Fellowship was established by the estate of William P. Van Wagenen, MD, founder and the first president of the Harvey Cushing Society, now the American Association of Neurological Surgeons (AANS). Awarded annually, this prestigious fellowship provides a stipend for study and research in a foreign country for a period of 12 months, with an optional family travel allowance. In addition, research support is available to the university, hospital, or laboratory which has agreed to sponsor the Van Wagenen Fellow. The Van Wagenen Fellowship gives freedom in scientific and clinical development without the limitations often imposed by many research grants and fellowship.

Past Fellows
Richard M. Bergland, MD (1968)
John M. Tew Jr., MD (1969)
M. Peter Heilbrun, MD (1970)
Ira D. Denton Jr., MD (1971)
Robert A. Ratcheson, MD (1972)
Joan L. Venes, MD (1973)
W. Michael Vise, MD (1974)
Lawrence H. Pitts, MD (1975)
Patrick J. Kelly, MD (1976)
William F. Chandler, MD (1977)
Jay D. Law, MD (1978)
George W. Tyson, MD, MBA (1979)
L. Dade Lunsford, MD (1980)
Stephen J. Haines, MD (1981)
Larry V. Carson, MD, MBA (1982)
Lawrence F. Borges, MD (1983)
Edmund H. Frank, MD (1984)

Marc R. Mayberg, MD (1985)

Edward G. Hames III, MD, PhD (1986)

Emily D. Friedman, MD (1987)

Mark W. Jones, MD (1988)

David W. Newell, MD (1989)

Walter A. Hall, MD (1990)

Ian F. Pollack, MD (1991)

Mary Louise Hlavin, MD (1992)

Mark E. Linskey, MD (1993)

Ivar M. Mendez, MD, PhD (1994)

Timothy C. Ryken, MD (1995)

Howard L. Weiner, MD (1996)

Zelma H. T. Kiss, MD, PhD (1997)

Kamal Thapar, MD (1998)

Theodore Schwartz, MD (1999)

P. Charles Garell, MD (2000)

Shekar N. Kurpad, MD, PhD (2001)

Saadi Ghatan, MD (2002)

Odette A. Harris, MD (2003)

Stephen M. Russell, MD (2004)

Devin K. Binder, MD, PhD (2005)

Uzma Samadani, MD, PhD (2006)

Yu-Hung Kuo, MD, PhD (2006)

James C. Miller, MD (2007)

Young Neurosurgeons' Committee Public Service Citation Awardees

IN 2001, THE AANS BOARD OF DIRECTORS established a Young Neurosurgeons' Committee Public Service Citation. This citation recognizes and honors the extraordinary efforts of a young neurosurgeon who, outside the traditional art and science of neurosurgery, has served the public in an exemplary fashion and thereby brings both greater benefit to mankind and greater honor to our specialty. The awardees:

Carl Lauryssen, MD, for development of a neurosurgical medical mission in Nairobi (2001).

Nicholas Boulis, MD, for his efforts in bringing neurosurgical care to Guatemala (2002).

Daniel F. Kelly, MD, for meritorious service in promoting and culturing international cooperation with FIENS and FIND (2003).

Rahul Jandial, MD, for establishing the International Neurosurgical Children's Association with the purpose of providing international hospitals with needed equipment and staff training (2004).

Rocco A. Armonda, MD, for his extraordinary public service during his tour of duty as the commander of the 207th Neurosurgical Team in Iraq (2005).

Mark R. McLaughlin, MD, for his efforts in facilitating funding, housing, accommodations and training for Russian neurosurgeons in various centers in the United States (2006).

AANS Executive Directors

Carl H. Hauber, CAE, JD
1977–1996

Robert E. Draba, PhD
1996–1998

Dave Fellers
1999–2000

Thomas A. Marshall
2000–

Publications (year published)

Self Assessment in Neurological Surgery (SANS) *I, II, III, IV, V, VI* by AANS/CNS (1978–1997)

History of the American Association of Neurological Surgeons founded in 1931 as The Harvey Cushing Society: 1931–1981 by AANS (1981)

Great Men With Sick Brains and Other Essays [out of print] by Bengt Ljunggren, MD (1989)

Intracranial Vascular Malformations [out of print] by Daniel L. Barrow, MD (1990)

Malignant Cerebral Glioma [out of print] by Michael L. J. Apuzzo, MD (1990)

Management of Posttraumatic Spinal Instability [out of print] by Paul R. Cooper, MD (1990)

Neurosurgical Treatment of Disorders of the Thoracic Spine [out of print] by Edward C. Tarlov, MD (1990)

Complications and Sequelae of Head Injury by Daniel L. Barrow, MD (1991)

Complications of Spinal Surgery [out of print] by Edward C. Tarlov, MD (1991)

Contemporary Diagnosis and Management of Pituitary Adenomas [out of print] by Paul R. Cooper, MD (1991)

Neurosurgical Aspects of Epilepsy by Michael L. J. Apuzzo, MD (1991)

The Neuroanatomy of Leonardo da Vinci [out of print] by Edwin M. Todd, MD (1991)

Neurosurgical Operative Atlas, Volumes I through 9 [Volumes 5 and 8 are out of print] by Setti S. Rengachary, MD, and Robert H. Wilkins, MD (1991)–(2000)

Cerebrovascular Occlusive Disease and Brain Ischemia [out of print] by Issam A. Awad, MD (1992)

Degenerative Disease of the Cervical Spine [out of print] by Paul R. Cooper, MD (1992)

Neurosurgery for the Third Millennium by Michael L. J. Apuzzo, MD (1992)

Neurosurgical Classics by Robert H. Wilkins, MD (1992)

Practical Approaches to Peripheral Nerve Surgery [out of print] by Edward C. Benzel, MD (1992)

The Surgical Art of Harvey Cushing [out of print] by Peter McL. Black, MD (1992)

Cavernous Malformations by Issam A. Awad, MD, and Daniel L. Barrow, MD (1993)

Current Management of Cerebral Aneurysms by Issam A. Awad, MD, and Daniel L. Barrow, MD (1993)

Harvey Cushing at the Brigham by Peter McL. Black, MD, PhD, Matthew R. Moore, MD, and Eugene Rossitch Jr., MD (1993)

Interactive Image-Guided Neurosurgery by Robert J. Maciunas, MD (1993)

Neurosurgical Emergencies, Volume I [out of print] by Christopher M. Loftus, MD (1993)

Spinal Instrumentation [out of print] by Deborah L. Benzil, MD (1993)

Spinal Trauma: Current Evaluation & Management by Gary L. Rea, MD, and Carole A. Miller, MD (1993)

Surgery of the Cranial Nerves of the Posterior Fossa by Daniel L. Barrow, MD (1993)

Contemporary Management of Spinal Cord Injury by Charles H. Tator, MD, and Edward C. Benzel, MD (1994)

Criteria for the Review of Neurosurgical Procedures [out of print] by Robert E. Florin, MD (1994)

Dural Arteriovenous Malformation [out of print] by Issam A. Awad, MD (1994)

Neurosurgical Emergencies, Volume II by Christopher M. Loftus, MD (1994)

Philosophy of Neurological Surgery by Issam A. Awad, MD (1994)

Spine Tumors [out of print] by Gary L. Rea, MD (1994)

Benign Cerebral Gliomas, Volume I and 2 by Michael L. J. Apuzzo, MD (1995)

Endovascular Neurological Intervention by Robert J. Maciunas, MD (1995)

Giant Intracranial Aneurysms by Issam A. Awad, MD, and Daniel L. Barrow, MD (1995)

Neurosurgical Aspects of Pregnancy by Christopher M. Loftus, MD (1995)

Surgical Exposure of the Spine: An Extensile Approach [out of print] by Edward C. Benzel, MD (1995)

Subarachnoid Hemorrhage: Pathophysiology and Man by Joshua B. Bederson, MD (1996)

Tethered Cord Syndrome [out of print] by Shokei Yamada, MD, PhD, FACS (1996)

The DREZ Operation by Blaine S. Nashold Jr., MD, Robert D. Pearlstein, PhD, and Allan H. Friedman, MD (1996)

A History of Neurosurgery by Samuel H. Greenblatt, MD, T. Forcht Dagi, MD, and Mel H. Epstein, MD (1997)

Cerebrospinal Fluid Collections by Howard H. Kaufman, MD (1997)

Neurological Classics, 2nd Edition by Robert H. Wilkins, MD, and Irwin A. Brody, MD (1997)

Nuances of Neurosurgical Technique, 2nd Edition by Milton D. Heifetz, MD (1997)

Pediatric Neurosurgical Intensive Care by Brian T. Andrews, MD, FACS, and Gregory B. Hammer, MD (1997)

Physician's Perspective on Medical Law, Volume I and II [out of print] by Howard H. Kaufman, MD (1997)

Syringomyelia and the Chiari Malformation by John A. Anson, MD, Edward C. Benzel, MD, and Issam A. Awad, MD (1997)

Advanced Techniques in Central Nervous System Metastases by Robert J. Maciunas, MD (1998)

Calvarial & Dural Reconstruction by Setti S. Rengachary, MD, and Edward C. Benzel, MD (1998)

Guide to the Primary Care of Neurological Disorders by A. John Popp, MD (1998)

Peripheral Nerve Injuries, 2nd Edition by Webb Haymaker, MD, and Barnes Woodhall, MD (1998)

The Genesis of Neuroscience by A. Earl Walker, MD, Edited by Edward R. Laws Jr., MD, and George B. Udvarhelyi, MD (1998)

Treatment of Carotid Disorders: Practitioner's Manual by Joshua B. Bederson, MD; Stanley Tuhrim, MD (1998)

Intracranial Endoscopic Neurosurgery by David F. Jimenez, MD (1999)

LINAC and Gamma Knife Radiosurgery by Isabelle M. Germano, MD (1999)

Missile Wounds of the Head & Neck, Volume I by Bizhan Aarabi, MD, and Howard H. Kaufman, MD (1999)

Neurosurgical Care of the Elderly by Warren R. Selman, MD, and Edward C. Benzel, MD (1999)

Infections in Neurosurgery by Walter A. Hall, MD, and Ian E. McCutcheon, MD (2000)

Management and Prognosis of Severe Traumatic Brain Injury by the Brain Trauma Foundation and the American Association of Neurological Surgeons (2000)

Neural Prostheses, Reversing the Vector of Surgery by Robert J. Maciunas, MD (2000)

Neurosurgical Classics II by Robert H. Wilkins, MD, and Gloria K. Wilkins (2000)

AANS Guide to Informed Consent by AANS (2001)

AANS Health Insurance Portability and Accountability Act (HIPAA) Privacy Manual by AANS (2001)

Moyamoya Disease by Kiyonobu Ikezaki, MD, PhD, and Christopher M. Loftus, MD, FACS (2001)

Surgical Management of Low Back Pain by Daniel K. Resnick, MD, and Regis Haid, MD (2001)

Biomechanics of Spine Stabilization by Edward C. Benzel, MD (2002)

Innovations in Spinal Fixation Module I: Thoracic Instrumentation (DVD) by AANS (2002)

Innovations in Spinal Fixation Module II: Lumbar/Sacral/Pelvic Instrumentation (DVD) by Christopher I. Shaffrey, MD (2002)

Missile Wounds of the Head & Neck, Volume II by Bizhan Aarabi, MD, and Howard H. Kaufman, MD (2002)

Neurological Sports Medicine by Julian E. Bailes, MD, and Arthur L. Day, MD (2002)

Neurosurgical Treatment of Movement Disorders by Isabelle M. Germano, MD (2002)

Signs, Syndromes, & Eponyms by Timir Banerjee, MD, and Alvaro A. Domingues da Silva, MD (2002)

Spinal Vascular Malformations by Daniel L. Barrow, MD, and Issam A. Awad, MD (2002)

Intensive Care in Neurosurgery by Brian T. Andrews, MD, FACS (2003)

The Operating Room for the 21st Century by Michael L. J. Apuzzo, MD (2003)

AANS Health Insurance Portability and Accountability Act (HIPAA) Security Manual by AANS (2004)

Minimally Invasive Spinal Techniques (DVD) by Mick J. Perez-Cruet, MD, and Robert F. Heary, MD (2004)

Improving Your Bottom Line in Today's Neurosurgical Practice (DVD) by James I. Ausman, MD, PhD (2005)

Medical Liability: How to Develop an Action Plan (DVD) by John A. Kusske, MD (2005 + 2007)

Neurosurgeon's E&M Reference Card by AANS (2005, 2007)

Preparation for Medical/Legal Testimony DVD by Stanley W. Fronczak, MD, JD, FACS (2005)

Update on Tumors for the General Neurosurgeon (DVD) by Jeffrey N. Bruce, MD, FACS (2005)

* *Vertebroplasty and Kyphoplasty* by Daniel K. Resnick, MD, and Steven Garfin, MD (2005)

AANS Express Code: Quick Reference to ICD-9 Coding by AANS (2006)

AANS Guide to Coding: Mastering the Global Service Package for Neurological Surgery Services by AANS (2006, 2007)

Cerebral Trauma State-of-the-Art Treatment (DVD) by Alex B. Valadka, MD (2006)

* *Controversies in Neurological Surgery* by Michael T. Lawton, MD, Daryl R. Gress, MD, and Randall T. Higashida, MD (2006)

Head Trauma: Current Treatments and Controversies (DVD) by Geoffrey T. Manley, MD, PhD, and Shelly D. Timmons, MD, PhD (2006)

Minimally Invasive Microendoscopic Discectomy (DVD) by Kevin T. Foley, MD (2006)

Modern Techniques and Future Trends in Lumbar Interbody Fusion (DVD) by Robert F. Heary, MD, and Eric J. Woodard, MD (2006)

* *Neurosurgical Operative Atlas: Neuro-Oncology* by Behnam Badie, MD (2007)

* *Neurosurgical Operative Atlas: Spine & Peripheral Nerves* by Setti S. Rengachary, MD (2007)

* *The Legacy of Harvey Cushing: Profiles of Patient Care* by Aaron A. Cohen-Gadol, MD and Dennis D. Spencer, MD (2007)

* *A Guide to the Primary Care of Neurological Disorders, 2ⁿᵈ Edition*, A. John Popp, MD (scheduled for June 2007)

* *Neurosurgical Emergencies, 2ⁿᵈ Edition*, Christopher A. Loftus, MD (scheduled for September 2007)

* Co-published with Thieme Medical Publishers

Leaders in Neuroscience Video Interviews

In 1980, a series of 10 videotaped oral histories were produced for the 50th Anniversary Meeting of The American Association of Neurological Surgeons. The histories were primarily of those who had trained with, or who had known, Harvey Cushing and other early neurosurgeons. Subsequently, the program was expanded to include additional neurosurgeons, neurologists, and individuals in the neurosciences both in North America and internationally.

Archives Committee members believed that it is important to document the biographies of eminent neuroscientists throughout the world who have made significant and critical contributions to the understanding and treatment of the normal and abnormal functions of the brain. These video oral histories afford the viewer an intimate opportunity to learn of a doctor's early education, of influential teachers, research activities, acquaintances, and friendships with outstanding physicians, surgeons, and scientists. Together, these "firsthand" accounts constitute an eye-witness history of the evolving neurosurgical specialty.

Non-neurosurgeons in the series include specialists in neurology, neuropathology, psychopharmacology, neurophthalmology, neuro-radiology, visual physiology, otolaryngology, neurophysiology, and nuclear medicine. Non-physicians in the series include Cushing's medical artist, the founder of neuroscience nurse training, the engineer who designed the first shunt for hydrocephalus, and the medical archivist at Codman & Shurtleff.

For an annotated catalog of the *Leaders in Neuroscience* program, please go to http://www.neurosurgery.org/cybermuseum/giftshop/abstract.html.

Raymond D. Adams, MD (1989)

Adelola Adeloye, MD (1991)

Eben Alexander Jr., MD (1994)

Orlando Andy, MD (1992)

Anna A. Artaryan, MD (1991)

Julius Axelrod, PhD (1990)

Orville T. Bailey, MD (1991)

Louis Bakay, MD (1992)

H. Thomas Ballantine, MD (1989)

Carl Gustaf Bernhard, MD (1995)

Claude Bertrand, MD (1993)

Anders Bjorklund, MD (1993)

Edwin Boldrey, MD (1988)

Louis D. Boshes, MD (1992)

Mario Brock, MD (1993)

Paul Bucy, MD (1981)

Max Chamlin, MD (1991)

Jacob Chandy, MD (1991)

Shelley N. Chou, MD, PhD (1994)

W. Kemp Clark, MD (1985)

Ralph B. Cloward, MD (1991)

Mildred Codding (1990)

Cushing's (2000th) Verified Brain Tumor Operation (1981)

Loyal Davis, MD (1981)

Richard L. DeSaussure, Jr., MD (1988)

Giovanni DiChiro, MD (1990)

Donald Dohn, MD (1993)

Vinko Dolenc, MD (1992)

Robert S. Dow, MD (1991)

Charles G. Drake, MD (1995)

C. Miller Fisher, MD (1995)

Eldon L. Foltz, MD (1991)

Lyle A. French, MD (1988)

J. Garber Galbraith, MD (1985)

W. James Gardner, MD (1981)

William J. German, MD (1981)

Philip Gildenberg, MD (1991)

Sidney Goldring, MD (1991)

Nicholas Gotten, MD (1992)

John Green, MD (1988)

Torgney Greitz, MD, PhD (1995)

Robert L. Grubb, MD (1992)

Wallace B. Hamby, MD (1989)

Jules Hardy, MD (1991)

Robert Heath, MD (1989)

Francis X. Herr (1993)

John Holter, DSc (1989)

William F. House, MD (1991)

David Hubel, MD (1994)

William E. Hunt, MD (1992)

Ruth Kerr Jakoby, MD, FACS, JD (1994)

John Jane, MD (1994)

Herbert H. Jasper, MD (1993)

Bryan Jennett, MD (1993)

Edgar A. Kahn, MD (1981)

Seymour Kety, MD (1990)

Robert B. King, MD (1991)

Yorvan Kiryabwire, MD (1991)

Alexander N. Konovalov, MD (1991)

Theodore Kurze, MD (1992)

John H. Lawrence, MD (1991)

Jacques LeBeau, MD (1993)

F. Laurence Levy, MD (1991)

Richard U. Light, MD (1981)

Leonid B. Likhterman, MD (1991)

Robert B. Livingston, MD (1994)

Collin S. MacCarty, MD (1988)

Paul MacLean, MD (1990)

H. W. Magoun, PhD (1988)

Vernon Mark, MD (1990)

Antonio Marques, MD (1989)

Agnes Marshall, RN (1991)

Frank H. Mayfield, MD (1981)

William W. McKinney, MD (1989)

William F. Meacham, MD (1988)

Russell Meyers, MD (1990)

Guram O. Mjavanadze, MD (1991)

Thomas P. Morley, MD (1994)

Lester A. Mount, MD (1985)

Vernon B. Mountcastle, MD (1993)

Frances Murphey, MD (1988)

Walle H. J. Nauta, MD (1990)

Guy L. Odom, MD (1981)

Robert G. Ojemann, MD (1991)

Eric Oldberg, MD (1981)

Irvine H. Page, MD (1988)

Sanford Palay, MD (1993)

Dwight Parkinson, MD (1988)

Emil Pasztor, MD (1991)

Russel Patterson, MD (1991)

Bernard Pertuiset, MD (1993)

Byron C. Pevehouse, MD (1994)

Urban Ponten, MD, PhD (1995)

Lawrence J. Pool, MD (1988)

Karl Pribram, MD (1993)

Robert H. Pudenz (1991)

Marcus E. Raichle, MD (1995)

Brigadier Ramamurthi, MD (1993)

Robert Rand, MD (1991)

Bronson S. Ray, MD (1981)

Hugo Rizzoli, MD (1988)

Andrei P. Romodanov, MD (1991)

Daniel Ruge, MD (1988)

Gerishom Sande, MD (1991)

Keiji Sano, MD (1985)

Richard C. Schneider, MD (1985)

Kurt Schurmann, MD (1992)

Henry G. Schwartz, MD (1988)

R. Eustace Semmes, MD (1988)

Frank P. Smith, MD (1992)

Louis Sokoloff, MD (1990)

Ladislau Steiner, MD (1994)

W. Eugene Stern, MD (1991)

Oscar Sugar, MD (1993)

Thoralf M. Sundt, MD (1985)

William H. Sweet, MD (1989)

Lindsay Symon, MD (1988 + 1991)

Jean Talairach, MD (1994)

Juan M. Taveras, MD (1991)

Owsei Temkin, MD (1988)

Edwin Todd, MD (1991)

Charles E. Troland, MD (1989)

A. Roy Tyrer, MD (1992)

George B. Udvarhelyi, MD (1993)

Henk Verbiest, MD (1991)

Siegfried Vogel, MD (1991)

H. Alfons Walder, MD (1988)

A. Earl Walker, MD (1991)

Arthur A. Ward, Jr., MD (1991)

Robert Watson, MD (1991)

James Watts, MD (1989)

Frank Wrenn, MD (1989)

Gazi Yasargil, MD (1988)

Harry M. Zimmerman, MD (1988)

AANS Logos and their Origins

Photograph of Dr. Cushing taken in France by Arnold Klebs in 1931.

AANS Logo 1966 to 1997

American Association of Neurological Surgeons

John Singer Sargent charcoal sketch of Harvey Cushing, 1916. This sketch was used to design the Cushing 45-cent stamp in 1988 and became the image for the AANS logo in 1997.

Above: The scientific program committee strives to make each annual meeting innovative; in 2004 attendees enjoyed sessions in 3-D.

Right and below: The first annual meeting of the Harvey Cushing Society was attended by 23 prominent surgeons. Today, the AANS Annual Meeting draws 2,500-3,000 medical attendees and more than 230 exhibiting companies.

In addition to plenary sessions and didactic lectures delivered during breakfast seminars, the AANS Annual Meeting also offers hands-on practical clinics and educational posters for viewing.

Meeting attendees participate in free sessions that help them keep up with technology. Offered in the AANS Resource Center in the exhibit hall, these sessions taught attendees Power Point for speaking presentations, how to use the Internet, how to capture digital photographs in the OR, or use PDA's in their daily practice.

The Silent Auction is championed by the AANS Young Neurosurgeon's Committee as a benefit for the Neurosurgery Research and Education Foundation (NREF). Here, meeting attendees are checking their entries to make sure they haven't been outbid. First introduced in 1998, the auction typically raises between $25,000 and $30,000 to help fund important neurosurgical research through the NREF grant program.

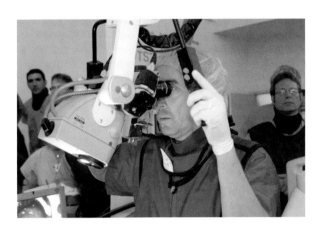

AANS teaches the most advanced, innovative neurosurgical techniques through *Master Series* courses. These neurosurgeons are learning minimally invasive spinal techniques in a cadaver clinic.

AANS Members must demonstrate 60 hours of Category I CME over three years to maintain membership in the AANS.

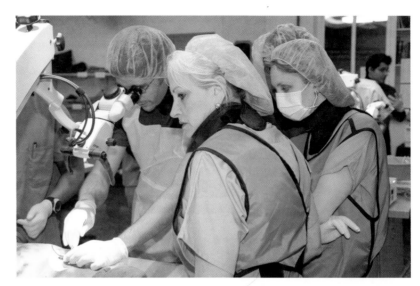

AANS educational activities extend beyond neurosurgeons; the organization actively involves physician assistants, nurses and other neurosurgical practitioners to advance their neurosurgical training.

An important priority for AANS is resident education. Here, residents selected by their program directors learn pediatric neurosurgical techniques.